Talking Toxicology

RECOGNIZING, UNDERSTANDING & REDUCING TOXIC EXPOSURES

NOREEN KHAN-MAYBERRY, PhD

DEDICATION

Dedicated to my late mother

Nicole Marie Gabriel

A beautiful angel who was taken far too soon.
Your spirit is unmatched, yet your legacy lives on.
I love and miss you every day.

NOTE TO READERS

This book is meant to be a relatively easy to understand guide for laypersons to gain insight into toxicology and how this science is an integral part of our daily life. While this book will allow you to gain an understanding of toxicology, it is not meant to be a comprehensive guide for those studying to become toxicologists.

In addition, the statements contained in this book are not intended to treat, diagnose or cure any medical conditions. Your physician should be consulted about any health issues or concerns. If you suspect environmental contamination in your home consult a professional that can provide a toxicological assessment.

The opinions expressed herein are solely those of the author and do not necessarily reflect the views of NASA or the federal government.

Toxicology that you can understand – straight from a Toxicologist

CONTENTS

ACKNOWLEDGMENTS

For my husband, soul mate, and best friend Chris and our beautiful princess Nicole. Words cannot adequately express my love for you and our family.

A special thank you to my father, M.Y. Khan, a wonderful man who has always traveled his own path and is a true inspiration to me.

To all of my dear family & true friends scattered around the globe, I love you. To the many professors and mentors who took the time to impart academic knowledge and wisdom – I am truly grateful. To Dr. Tony O'Donnell, who inspired me to put my gifts on paper. Thank you!

This work is not possible without God who has given me everything.

SO HOW TOXIC AM I?

Every day we are inundated with toxic exposures coming at us from seemingly every direction. These toxic exposures range from the *air* that we breathe, the *water* that we drink and bathe in, and the *foods* that we consume harvested from *soils* that may be saturated with agriculturally applied chemicals, and contaminated by *runoff water* which contains toxic compounds. Our public drinking water also contains chemical by-products, some of which are formed by the very chemical treatment that is meant to disinfect our drinking water. We breathe countless unknown chemical mixtures in our air – some of these toxic exposures are natural in origin while others develop as a result of man-made processes. We continuously place a large toll on our body due to these multiple exposures. Fortunately, our body has been designed perfectly to combat toxic exposures – be them from natural sources (toxins) or man-made (toxicants). However, a body, like any machine or man-made system, can become overloaded and toxic effects can manifest in the form of symptoms or, even worse, disease.

So how toxic are you? Well the answer depends on your environment, habits and your genetics, stress level, health, lifestyle and dietary habits. While we have little control over many of the sources of toxic exposures, we can do something to reduce some of our toxic exposures as well as assist our body in dealing with and eliminating the numerous toxic chemicals that we routinely encounter.

In order to understand how to reduce our exposure to a variety of toxic environmental factors, we must first educate ourselves in key areas of toxicology. You have made the first step by reading this book.

While reading this book you should be able to answer the following questions:

(1)   What are toxins and toxicants? What is the difference?

(2)   How do dosage, duration and potency of toxic exposures determine symptoms of toxicity?

(3)   What are the sources of toxic exposures?

(4)   How does our body process and deal with toxic exposures?

(5)   What are the short-term and long-term risks from toxicity?

(6)   How can I reduce my exposure to toxins and toxicants?

(7)   What can I do to speed up the removal of toxins and toxicants from my body?

Remember that a poison can be anything that is capable of causing a harmful response in a biological system. Every known chemical has the potential to cause injury or death if the dosage (amount) is sufficient. Hence the quote from *Paracelsus* (the Father of Toxicology), "All substances are poisons; there is none which is not a poison. The right dose differentiates a poison from a remedy."

While many things may appear to be out of our control, your life is still full of choices. You can choose to react or you can choose to stay the same. You can choose to take action and improve your environment and health. We all have a start date and an end date, the "dash" is what we are living right now. The choice and the power are in your hands to improve the quality of your dash by reducing toxicity in your life!

-Dr. Noreen

1 WHAT ARE TOXINS AND TOXICANTS?

Toxic exposures, or exposures to potentially poisonous compounds, can stem from organic (biological) or inorganic (man-made or non-living) sources. Stedman's Medical Dictionary (24th edition) defines a toxin as a noxious or poisonous substance that is formed either (1) as an essential part of the cell or tissue, (2) as a product from outside the cell (exotoxin), (3) or as a combination of the two, during the metabolism and growth of certain microorganisms, as well as some of the higher plant and animal species. This is a long and complex definition for most laypersons.

So really, what does this long definition mean? Toxins <u>are natural</u> they are not manufactured or man-made. Toxins can be from a natural source from outside of the body, or they can be produced inside of the body. A toxin can come from a tissue within the body or it can be introduced from an external source, such as ingesting bacteria contaminated foods or inhaling high concentrations of airborne mycotoxin-producing mold spores. In general, toxins are relatively complex antigenic (they stimulate an immune response) molecules, and their chemical compositions are usually not precisely known. Something is antigenic when the body recognizes that it is "foreign" or does not belong. The immune system will respond appropriately (produce an antibody) to deal with the foreign chemical(s). Bottom line is that Toxicologists classify toxins as those having a **biological** or **living** origin.

Toxicants are usually defined as **non-natural** chemical or chemical by-products that are created from man-made activities (anthropogenic sources). Toxicants can be manufactured, such as drugs developed in a laboratory, or they can be introduced into the environment through an event, such as a volcano driving chemical compounds into the air. Toxicants can also be introduced into the environment by everyday activities such as vehicle emissions, industrial emissions and runoff of chemical-containing liquids into water sources.

A toxicant, is also defined as anything that elicits a toxic response, hence this would include biologically-based toxins. The **accurate** way to refer to *all toxic chemicals collectively* is that they are <u>toxicants</u> or <u>toxics</u> (short-form). What you will read, see and hear in the media most often will be the terms "toxin" and "toxins" in reference to any poisonous chemical or class of chemicals. This is not a correct use of the term toxin, but it is how the word is used most often.

Remember the difference!

Toxin = toxic chemical from a biological source or produced by a biological system

Toxicant = (1) All toxic chemicals that cause a toxic response in the body (2) Toxic chemicals from a man-made origin or human activities

How do I recognize a toxic chemical?

Toxic agents (chemical or biological in origin) can come in a variety of forms. Solid, liquid or gaseous – basically any physical form that you can

Chapter 1 – What are Toxins & Toxicants?

imagine a chemical can be made into *and* it can be potentially toxic. So how do you recognize a toxic agent (toxics)? This is not always easy. There are the obvious forms like particulate matter (solid particles) that you can see, but what about the particles that are too small for you to see? Those smaller particles can be very toxic depending upon the type or chemistry of the toxin or toxicants in the particles. The size can greatly affect how toxic or safe the particle will be, this is largely due to the fact that the size will dictate how deeply the particle will penetrate into the respiratory airway.

Then there are also liquid toxics. These dissolved or liquid toxins and toxicants can either be more readily absorbed becoming more toxic, or less readily absorbed by the body rendering them less toxic. Gaseous or toxic agents that are in vaporized forms are generally inhaled and can cause damage, again depending upon their chemistry and concentration (dosage) that you are exposed to. Vapors or gases can be difficult to recognize, or they can be relatively easy to see (picture gasoline vapors rising as you pump gas into your vehicle) yet difficult to avoid due to our habits.

You are getting a glimpse of how confusing recognizing toxic agents can be. Simply put, it is not so easy to recognize toxic agents in our everyday life, even for a trained toxicologist! Is it starting to make sense as to why Toxicology is a science? With so many types of toxins and toxicants in our vast universe, it is important that we strive to understand what we can about these toxic agents and the roles they play in our life.

Toxicology is the study of poisons. By studying toxicology we look at the effect of toxic poisons on the body and the environment; this combines scientific knowledge from biology, chemistry, pharmacology and medicine. This medical science affects our health by direct contact or indirectly through the contamination of environmental factors (air, water, soil and wind) and our foods that we consume.

There are many specialties in the field of toxicology that allow the Toxicologist to specialize on certain aspect(s) of toxicology. Some examples include Mechanistic Toxicologists, Regulatory Toxicologists, Environmental Toxicologists, Food Toxicologists, and the list goes on. The first word in the title indicates the type of toxicologist and the general area of their specialty.

Toxicologists can hold several types of degrees, most commonly you will find that they have obtained a PhD, MD or DVM, which indicates the highest level of education in the field. There are also toxicologists with Master's level degrees that work alongside professional/doctoral level toxicologists or on their own. Toxicologists work in a wide variety of fields and industries (medical, chemical, petrochemical, pharmaceutical, government, public health, consulting). The wide variety of roles that a Toxicologist can play makes the science of toxicology integral across public and private industries.

Chapter Summary

It has become all too frequent to either hear about toxicology tests in the media or read and hear that practically everything is toxic. The dose can and will make the difference in toxicity, so in essence just about anything can be toxic. As an informed consumer and simply as a member of human race, it is so vitally important that you have decided to show an interest in Toxicology and understand how toxicity affects your quality of life.

2 TOXICITY: A PART OF LIFE & THE CONSEQUENCE OF HOW WE LIVE

Every year, people die from toxic exposures. Many of them may die from cancer or another chronic disease that stemmed from exposure to a toxic agent or to toxic mixtures. Because the types of toxins and toxicants are so varied in nature, it is virtually impossible to quantify the number of people that have gotten sick or died from a single toxic exposure or from long-term contact with toxins and toxicants.

The sources of toxicity are abundant and are ever-present in our homes, vehicles, offices as well as our outdoor work/play environments. At home we can look in almost any room and find toxic chemicals that we have purchased and intentionally brought into our indoor environment. Examples include cleaning products, laundry chemicals, paints, thinners, hydrocarbons and petroleum products, personal hygiene products, chemically treated fabrics, fire retardants, sealants, pesticides, pool chemicals and the list goes on. Generally speaking, people have many more toxins and toxicants than can be listed in a short paragraph. It can seem overwhelming when going through a list of potentially toxic chemicals. But many of us have learned to live with so many chemicals, that we may become complacent of their potential toxicity or we may cling to them as if they are part of their heritage and culture. Do you know anyone that cannot live without their bleach? I know far too many people, who do not believe that their house is clean unless they can smell the chemicals and they refuse to give up any chemical cleaners in the home. What is unfortunate is that as they are breathing in unmeasured concentrations of these household chemicals – this also means that they are getting untold dosages of volatile chemicals. They are also exposing their family and pets to the same potentially toxic environment. When you smell a chemical, or anything with a scent, this is a lightweight or volatile chemical which is evaporating into your breathable air. These repeated exposures to various toxic mixtures can lead to adverse health effects in the short-term such as headaches, nausea or fatigue and/or long-term effects such as chemical sensitivities, asthma, weight and mood changes or worse chronic disease.

Have you ever stopped to think about how many chemicals that you are exposed to every time that you enter into a new environment? I am not just talking about outdoors. I am referring to each space that you enter, in a vehicle, office, restaurant, store, hotel, etc. Each area contains a different set of chemical mixtures at varying concentrations. For the most part, they are harmless if you are not in these "spaces" for long periods of time. But what happens when you live or work in a contaminated space for months or years? Have you considered that your body is responding and may be slowly declining in its ability to deal with these long term exposures? A toxicologist makes these considerations. It is what this science is concerned with and why some of us work to set limits on the chemicals that can cause harm to human health. Toxicologists strive to protect people and the environment from harm caused by chemicals. While the effort is just, there is so much that is unknown about the synergistic (combined) effects of chemical mixtures. It is impossible to know and measure all of the types and concentrations of chemical mixtures since they are constantly changing due to natural and unnatural actions. This is why you should try to eliminate as many toxins and toxicants that are within your control. Conduct the following exercise and try to implement it on a routine basis (you decide the frequency, I recommend every 3-6 months).

Checklist of Common Household Toxicants: How many chemical roommates do you have in your home?

- Aerosols
- Air Fresheners/Deodorizers
- Bleaches (laundry, hair products)
- Detergents (dish-washing & laundry)
- Disinfectants
- Drain cleaners
- Fragrances (perfumes, scented oils, scented candles)
- General Household Cleaners
- Hair care (hairspray, hair dye, relaxers, permanent curls, heat protectors, shampoos, conditioners, styling products)
- Hair removal products
- Mothballs
- Moss Killers
- Oven cleaners
- Pesticides (insect, rodent, weed, fungicides)
- Polishes (shoes, furniture, automobile, metal)
- Paints (oil based, stains, spray)
- Paint removers (paint thinners, nail polish)
- Smoke (candles, tobacco)
- Vehicle maintenance chemicals (windshield fluid, oil, additives, antifreeze)
- Waxes (floor, automobile)

Total # _____

Chapter 2: Toxicity A Part of Life

How many of these toxic products can you eliminate from your home environment? List some below.

The Elimination List

1._____

2._____

3._____

4._____

5._____

How many of these toxic products have been in your home for years without being used? List some below.

The Toxic "Home-occupiers" List

1._____

2._____

3._____

4._____

5._____

Your inventory of chemicals at home is simply a list of the products that we intentionally invest our monies in and knowingly bring into our homes. Other environmental toxins and toxicants are mold toxins or mycotoxins (most commonly found toxins), radon, chemical emitting stone counter-tops and tiles, lead, carbon monoxide, cabinet and floor sealants, stain-repellent chemicals for drapery and furniture, dry cleaning chemicals and flame retardants on our clothing, furniture, drapery and bedding.

The Vehicle – Not just Transporting People

Private transportation revolutionized the way that people are able to live and travel. There are many chemicals "under the hood" that are inherent for the operation of a vehicle. We will not focus on those in this section. The car is not only transportation; it is a source of toxic exposure. Conduct the same type of toxic chemical inventory that you did in your home inside your car. How many chemicals are you storing in the vehicle? Have you ever tried to hold on to the new car smell as long as possible? Raise your hand if you are guilty. I was too and I must admit my brain was programmed to smell those chemicals and get a feeling of euphoria from having a nice "new" vehicle. Unfortunately, that nice new smell is called chemical offgassing and it is toxic.

A vehicle is full of chemical adhesives and sealants that contain many chemicals, but the primary one of concern in most cases (and one of the most harmful) is formaldehyde. The vehicle will offgas or emit the scent of these chemicals as they evaporate. You breathe them in every time you operate your vehicle. You may rarely recognize any symptoms from operating a new vehicle since you do have fresh air exchanges through your vents. However, the tighter the vehicle is designed, the longer the chemicals will remain. Many people will never open a window in order to preserve the scent for as long as possible. Over time the smell will dissipate as the amount of chemicals being offgassed dwindle down. Glue and sealants are not all that you are transporting with you! There are chemical treatments to the cloth, carpeting and leather materials throughout the vehicle. You also might use air fresheners in the car. These chemical fresheners come in a variety or scents and chemical mixtures. Some are sprayed on the fabric to offgas their scent and others are hung from the mirrors and now there are even oil-based clips that hang directly in front of your vents so that you can increase the amount that is emitted as you run the cooling and heating system. Let's journey to the trunk. Do you have coolant, tire dressings, water repellents, oil, gasoline additives or tire sealants in the trunk? You may not carry any of these, but if you do, is it really necessary to carry any or all of these chemicals?

The Office – Home of the industrial strength chemicals!

Is it surprising that so many people are getting sick? From a toxicologist's standpoint, no. From your standpoint, it probably is a little startling since so many of us take chemicals in our home for granted. And that's just inside your home! The office, where we work, or the schools in which we learn are full of chemicals that we personally cannot control. These places often get the majority of our time, depending upon the demands and schedules of work. If you try to conduct an inventory of chemicals at work you will find that many of them are similar to what was found on your personal inventory, the difference is that they are at a much stronger concentration. This is often referred to as "industrial strength". These higher concentrations are meant to protect the public from a wide variety of disease-causing bacteria, viruses and germs (toxins). You may or may not be in charge of the types of chemicals used by your maintenance staff, but you might find out if you ask. There are some chemicals that you may be able to eliminate from the office or school environment. If you can eliminate them – you probably should.

The Gym: Working off the weight, working in the chemicals

Many gyms pride themselves on having the latest equipment and facilities. Many customers demand state-of-the-art of fitness facilities. Often times, you can smell the chemicals that are being offgassed from various parts of the gym (workout equipment, mats, seating, etc). The equipment contains many chemicals and sealants that have formaldehyde as a major chemical component. There are also contaminants that are transmitted by sweat and other bodily fluids left on workout equipment and gym surfaces. Unfortunately, many of these places are not well ventilated and are air-conditioned in order to keep people who are working out as comfortable as possible. Consider asking how many fresh air exchanges the gym gets if you can smell chemicals for long periods of time.

Chapter Summary

It is important to consider your environment at all times. By becoming more aware of your "chemical surroundings" you may become more diligent about reducing the amount of time that you linger in areas with high concentrations of chemicals. You can also incorporate conducting a routine inventory (every 3-6 months) of the chemicals in your home and other places that you frequently occupy. Remember that you will not always smell chemicals and you should look for visual clues of chemical contamination or the presence of chemicals.

3 Routes of Toxicity

Our world is toxic! That cannot be refuted, even though some may try to downplay how toxic our environment is, or tone down the toxicity of what we interact with routinely. The previous chapter gave you a glimpse into toxins and toxicants that are a part of our everyday life. You may wonder how we are still functioning in this sea of toxicity. The answer varies depending upon the individual. However, we have the benefit of a perfectly designed body! The miracles that our bodies continuously work for us, 24 hours per day – 365 days per year, to combat the onslaught of repeated toxic exposures are amazing! In this chapter we will explore various aspects of the basics of toxicology including the routes of exposure, duration of exposure, dosage of toxins and toxicants, immediate versus delayed toxicity, and the range of toxic effects – all of which allow us to survive while living in a virtual sea of toxicity.

Routes of Toxic Exposure

A toxic chemical enters our body through major routes or pathways. These major routes include the lung (inhalation), the gastrointestinal tract (ingestion/eating), skin (dermal, topical, and percutaneous) and other parental routes (intravenous or intramuscular – direct injections).

Chapter 3: Routes of Toxicity

The following list shows routes of toxic exposure from the most effective to the least effective:

1. **Inhalation** (most effective)
2. **Intraperitoneal** (direct injection into the peritoneum, i.e., body cavity membrane that lines the abdominal organs)
3. **Subcutaneous** (direct injection under the skin layers)
4. **Intramuscular** (direct injection into a muscle)
5. **Intradermal** (direct injection into the dermal/skin layers)
6. **Oral**
7. **Dermal** (least effective)

The material or "vehicle" in which the chemical is dissolved or carried in before it enters a route of exposure to the body will greatly affect how much of the toxic agent is absorbed and distributed and ultimately how toxic the effects will be on our body.

The Duration of Exposure

The duration of an exposure will influence how toxic the effects or symptoms will be in a biological system. The duration is simply the time period that a toxicant is in the body. Toxicologists classify the duration of exposure to toxins and toxicants by specific time frames.

An **acute** exposure is a single exposure or multiple exposures that occur in a time frame of less than 24 hours. Usually an acute exposure is one single exposure. When referring to an acute environmental exposure by inhalation, this is usually when a person(s) is being continuously exposed to a toxic substance for less than 24 hours in the real world. This differs from a toxicology inhalation study in which "acute" is generally 4 hours of continuous chemical exposure to a test subject by inhalation. Repeated exposures are broken down into 3 categories: subacute, subchronic and chronic. A **subacute** exposure is a repeated exposure for 1 month or less.

Subchronic is a repeated exposure that occurs for 1 – 3 months. **Chronic** exposures last longer than 3 months.

Exposure Category	Duration of Exposure
Acute	Single or multiple exposure(s) within a 24 hr period
Subacute	Multiple exposures for 1 month or less
Subchronic	Multiple exposures for 1-3 months
Chronic	Multiple exposures for more than 3 months

An individual's everyday exposures cannot be as clearly defined as with test subjects in a controlled toxicology study since we are exposed to a variety of unknown toxins, toxicants and chemical mixtures on a daily basis. However, these same terms are used to classify real-world exposures. For example, you can state that an environmental, home, or work exposure to known chemicals in terms of one of these duration categories. If you are exposed to elevated concentrations of molds in your home for 1 month or less, you have had a subacute exposure.

The severity of a toxic agent can vary widely based upon the duration of exposure. Some toxicants are not immediately toxic when the exposure is chronic and at a concentration (dose) that is not high enough to produce any visible symptoms. However, over time that same chronic exposure can elicit a toxic response in the form of disease. Other toxins or toxicants can bring about severe and rapid-onset of symptoms – if they are absorbed quickly and travel to their site or sites of toxicity in the body or biological system. It is important to note that even acute toxic chemicals can elicit a delayed response along with the immediate toxic effect(s). Chronic exposures can also bring on immediate (acute) toxic effects as well as long-term chronic effects.

Chapter 3: Routes of Toxicity

Factors that influence how toxic a chemical will be are based on (1) its contact time (duration) in the body, particularly at its target site(s) of toxicity (2) how many times the exposure occurs and (3) whether or not it is metabolized or biotransformed into another more (or less) toxic byproduct (4) and how quickly the body is able to eliminate it.

If you are exposed to a toxic agent every 4 hours and it takes your body 4 hours to eliminate the toxin or toxicant completely, you will not likely experience a toxic effect since it will not build up in your body. However, if this same chemical were only eliminated by half (50%) every 4 hours, you would eventually start to build up the amount (dose) of the toxic agent that is in your body. This will increase the duration of time that the chemical will remain in your body, since every 4 hours you would still have half of the original dose remaining in your body and you would be getting a "fresh" exposure that is adding more of the toxic agent to your body.

Let's demonstrate this scenario of increasing the **duration of exposure** using 2 mg as the dosage of chemical exposure every 4 hours and assume that **6 mg** is when your body starts experiencing visible symptoms.

Time 0 (original exposure) to 2 mg of toxic chemical

At 4 hours – 1 mg is eliminated (½ of original dose)	1 mg (remaining chemical) + 2 mg (new exposure) = 3 mg in the body
At 8 hours – 1 mg is eliminated (3 mg – 1 mg)	2 mg (remaining chemical) + 2 mg (new exposure)= 4 mg remains in the body
At 12 hours – 1 mg is eliminated (4 mg – 1 mg)	3 mg (remaining chemical) + 2 mg (new exposure) = 5 mg remains in the body
At 16 hours – 1 mg is eliminated (5 mg – 1 mg)	4 mg (remaining chemical) + 2 mg (new exposure) = **6 mg** remains in the body **(Symptoms appear!)**

Notice that at each time point you have a greater amount of chemical in your body with longer residence time or exposure duration. Your body is only able to eliminate 50% of the original 2 mg dose or 1 mg every 4 hours, which is the same time that a fresh exposure to another 2 mg occurs. In this scenario, symptoms would appear at 16 hours, but that does not rule out toxic effects occurring that show no visibly or physically apparent symptoms.

The Dosage

For a drug, it is important to administer the right dosage that will have a sufficient duration of exposure in the body to cause repair of the targeted damage. For an unwanted chemical exposure, you would ideally want the dosage or concentration that you are exposed to, to only remain for an effective duration and concentration (dosage) that would not cause damage or toxic effects in your body. This is a simple way to look at the premise behind limits that are set by regulatory agencies. The regulations are set to ensure that we are only allowed to be exposed to concentrations of chemicals in our environment and chemicals in our foods that have a low enough dosage and duration time so that toxic effects are not experienced by the population. The dose dictates toxicity and can be the difference between a chemical being beneficial or toxic. Anything at the right dosage can be toxic, even pure water. Therefore the dose plays a prominent role in toxicology.

Immediate and Delayed Toxicity

We discussed immediate and delayed toxicity briefly in the duration section. A toxic agent that has immediate toxicity shows effects that develop or occur rapidly after the exposure. Delayed effects are toxic symptoms that occur after a period of time. Some chemicals lay seemingly "dormant" in the body for years. This is referred to as the latency period. Cancer causing chemicals (carcinogens) have very long latency periods of

20-30 years after the initial exposure. This is why it is often so difficult to pinpoint what has caused cancer.

The Range of Toxicity

There is a broad spectrum or range of toxicity that is caused by exposure to toxins and toxicants. Drugs can have more than one effect, yet a drug is generally targeted to treat a specific symptom, which is the drug's therapeutic effect. The other effects are generally unwanted side-effects. Certain side effects may have a different, beneficial or therapeutic use. Some side-effects are so bad (or toxic) that they outweigh the benefit of the therapeutic effect. An example of a therapy in which severe toxic effects are allowed is for the treatment of cancers. Radiation and chemotherapy are therapeutic treatments for cancers that cause a range of mild, moderate and severe symptoms as well as a number of adverse (toxic) health effects to patients. These types of cancer therapies have varying degrees of success which depend upon the type of cancer and the stage of damage that has occurred in the body. However, even though the symptoms are severe, success from the cancer therapies are not guaranteed. These therapies are toxic to healthy cells as wells as cancerous cells. Radiation and chemotherapy has been, and continues to be, the preferred or chosen route for treatment in most countries and for most cancer patients. This is because despite the harsh toxic effects on the body, if survival of a terminal illness is the result, the severe symptoms are viewed by many as necessary for destruction of cancerous cells.

This example of cancer treatment demonstrates the range of toxic effects as well as the range of effectiveness that can occur. It also is an example of an ethical debate between preserving life and enduring the toxic effects of treatments. The range of toxicity for toxins and toxicants can be mild, moderate, severe or even non-detectable for days, months or years. The reason that toxic studies will target varying durations (time-spans) on a variety of doses is to try to determine or predict what will be toxic, how and where it will be toxic in a biological system and how to protect against toxicity.

Chapter Summary

In this chapter we examined how toxicity can vary based upon the route of chemical exposure, the duration that the chemical remains in the body and the dosage of the chemical. We also looked at immediate versus delayed toxicity and took a glimpse at the wide range of toxic effects. These are just some of the many factors that a toxicologist must consider when conducting a toxic risk assessment. For you personally, becoming aware of how these factors affect toxicity can influence your habits and help you reduce your toxic exposures.

4 Mechanisms of Toxicity: How toxins & toxicants can cause damage in the body

As we discussed in the previous chapter, the determining factors of how toxic a chemical will be to our bodies depends upon (1) the route of exposure (how it gains entry into our body), (2) the dosage (amount of a toxicant that we are exposed to) and (3) the duration that we are in contact with the toxicant (how long we are exposed to the toxic chemical). Toxicologist's have a saying that was coined by the father of Toxicology, *Paracelsus* (his birth name was Auroleus Phillipus Theostratus Bombastus von Hohenheim, 1493-1541), "Dosis sola facit venenum" which roughly translated states that "only the dose makes the poison". In other words, anything can be harmful at the right concentration.

Along with dosage, the toxicologist must consider the mechanism of toxicity which determines how much of the toxin or toxicant is absorbed by the body, how and where the chemical is distributed in the body, how the body metabolizes or biotransforms the chemical(s) and how much is excreted or eliminated by the body. Collectively, this is *chemical disposition* or toxicokinetics (TK) or pharmacokinetics (PK). TK and PK are the rate at which a chemical will enter the body and the fate of the chemical once it enters the body) which can be determined by ADME (Absorption, Distribution, Metabolism and Elimination). They are very similar, but the distinction is that TK are toxicology studies which are conducted to determine systemic chemical disposition and PK deals with doses of drugs that are meant to be in the therapeutic range. The toxicologist also calculates in safety factors that are usually meant to protect the most sensitive groups in the population. All of these factors ultimately dictate how toxic a chemical is determined to be and influences where regulations are set to protect us against these chemicals.

For example, let's look at a prescription or over-the-counter pain relief drug, if you take the prescribed dose, it is only effective if the medication is *absorbed* and is *distributed* (reaches) to its target site of action (the area of the body that is in pain or the site in the body that is signaling pain), and the drug remains effective long enough to remove the pain. The body must also be able to *metabolize* it or biotransform it into something that can be chemically effective and/or something that can be *eliminated* or removed from the body, and is not stored in the body for too long of a period. If the drug is eliminated too quickly, it will not be effective, or if the dosage is not high enough, there will be no pain relief. Finally, on its way out of the body (excretion), the chemical should be sufficiently removed. Throughout the process, the drug should have no or minimal adverse side-effects or unintended symptoms or toxicity.

Again, the route, dose and duration of exposure to a toxin or toxicant will greatly influence how toxic a chemical is to the structure or function of a living organism. For toxicological evaluation of a chemical, the toxic effects must be documented in order to assign the appropriate hazard and the degree of toxicity of a particular chemical. The mechanisms that are responsible for how a chemical interacts with a living organism must also be understood by the Toxicologist. Collectively, the Toxicologist will look at the (1) dose, duration and route of exposure, (2) how the toxin or toxicant interacts with target molecules, organs or systems and (3) how the organism deals with the toxic exposure. All of this will aid the Toxicologist in determining a chemical's ultimate toxicity.

The more steps that are involved in the path to toxicity, the more complex a toxin or toxicant is considered to be. Once a chemical arrives at (or is delivered to) its target (or multiple targets) of toxicity, the toxic agent will interact with the target in one or more ways. This interaction(s) will trigger alterations or disturbances to the cellular function or structure of the target. This will in turn set off repair mechanisms at molecular, cellular or tissue levels, when the disturbances exceed the repair capacity, or if the repair mechanism becomes non-functional, then toxicity ensues.

Simply put,
1. the toxic chemical enters your body,
2. it makes its way to the site in your body that it can cause damage to (target)
3. it alters normal function at that site
4. your body recognizes that an unusual change has occurred and begins defending itself from the foreign invader
5. when the toxic chemical exceeds your body's capacity to repair or remove it (you are at saturation pharmacokinetics), damage occurs which is known as toxicity.

Some examples of adverse health effects from toxins and toxicants following more complex routes are cancer, tissue death and fibrosis. Conversely, some toxic chemicals can be largely eliminated before a sufficient amount is absorbed or distributed in the body. These are considered non-toxic or low toxicity types of chemicals. Often times the original chemical is the agent that causes toxicity. However a chemical by-product or metabolite of the original toxicant can end up being the agent that ultimately causes toxicity to a living organism.

Assessing the Risk of Toxic Chemicals (Toxic Risk Assessment)

When toxicologists assess the risk of a chemical's ability to cause adverse effects on the health of people or on the safety of the environment, this is called a risk assessment. The toxicology risk assessment is based upon toxicology research data (toxicokinetics and/or pharmacokinetics) taken from several peer-reviewed studies that were conducted and/ or analyzed by a trained scientist and/or toxicologist. Limits that are set for exposures to hundreds of chemicals are based upon a risk assessment that considers scientific data, the route and likelihood of exposure to the chemical(s) or compound, and the severity of damage that the chemical(s) will cause. Regulatory agencies around the world that set varying limits do so based upon their expertise and the appropriate risk assessment. In the United States one of the first limits that was placed upon food was the Delany Clause in 1958, in which the US Congress mandated that the Food and Drug Administration (FDA) prohibit the addition of substances known to cause cancer in animals or humans.

Toxicokinetics – Absorption, Distribution, Metabolism, Elimination (ADME)

Absorption

Absorption is the transport of a chemical from the site of exposure, which is generally an external or internal body surface into the organism's circulation (systemic). Simply put it is the uptake of substances into or across tissues into the bloodstream. Toxins or toxicants may be absorbed by crossing the epithelial barriers such as (1) the epithelium of the skin, (2) thin cell layers of the lung or the GI tract, (3)the capillary endothelium, (4)the target organ or tissue, and will gain access to blood capillaries by diffusing through these cells. The rate at which chemicals are absorbed is affected by the concentration at the absorbing surface, the area of the absorbing surface, the rate or length of exposure and the dissolution capacity (how well it dissolves) of the chemical. Fat (lipid) solubility greatly influences how well a chemical will be absorbed. Most chemicals are highly fat soluble. Fat soluble toxins and toxicants are more readily absorbed, stored and accumulated than water-soluble substances. Many toxins and toxicants are absorbed by the intestines.

Presystemic Elimination

Toxic chemicals can be eliminated from the body during the process of transferring it from the entry site to the systemic circulation; thereby removing the chemical <u>before</u> it can get into the body's circulation. The gastrointestinal (GI) tract is largely responsible for pre-systemic elimination, since most chemicals that are ingested (consumed by eating or drinking), must pass through the GI's mucosal cells, the liver and the lung prior to being distributed to the rest of the body. GI mucosa and the liver may eliminate a large amount of the toxic chemical during its passage through these tissues, decreasing the amount that is available to be distributed into circulation. However, if a chemical toxin or toxicant has the GI mucosa, liver or lung as its target of toxicity, or if it is sufficiently toxic to harm these organs, even if they are not the intended targets, they can still cause enough damage (toxicity) during the pre-systemic elimination process and diminish the bodies capacity for future removal of any toxic chemical. One common example of a chemical that can cause pre-systemic damage is alcohol (ethanol) consumption.

Distribution

Toxins and toxicants are distributed into the blood (circulation) and enter the space between cells (extracellular space) and may penetrate into the cells. Toxic agents that dissolve in the water portion of the blood plasma can diffuse into the capillary endothelium (surface) through (1) spaces within cells, and (2) pores (fenestrae) in the cells and (3) across the cell's protective membrane.

Fat soluble toxins and toxicants easily move across the cells by diffusion (cell membranes are made of fat and like dissolves like). In contrast, water soluble or highly charged toxins or toxicants do not enter cells without specialized membrane transport systems that can transfer them into the interior of the cells. The distribution phase begins when chemicals arrive at their target site or target sites of toxicity, i.e., sites of action. In many cases the site of action is on the surface or the interior of a particular cell. Toxic chemicals can also interact with an enzyme within the cell to form the ultimate toxic agent. There are processes that aid in distribution of toxicants to the target site of toxicity and there are also opposing processes that the body has to move the chemical away from its site of action.

Distribution may be **enhanced** by four general processes:

1. Pore size: the pore size of the capillaries surface (endothelium); Liver and Kidneys have large pore sizes which favor the accumulation of chemicals in these organs
2. Transport systems: these are specialized membrane transport or carrier mediated uptake systems that distribute the toxicant to the site of action (examples: Sodium/Potassium pump, Voltage gated Calcium channels)
3. Organelles: accumulation of the chemical into specialized structures (organelles) within the cells where it can cause cellular dysfunction or cell death, and
4. Reversible intracellular binding: binding of a toxicant to a surface of the cell component and causing a reversal or release of previously bound toxicants or cellular dysfunction

Chapter 4: Mechanisms of Toxicity

Distribution may be **opposed** by five general processes:

1. <u>Binding to plasma proteins</u>: chemicals may adhere to plasma proteins that may be high molecular weight proteins or lipoproteins that cannot physically leave the plasma by diffusion; essentially trapping the toxicant at the protein and stopping further distribution

2. <u>Specialized barriers</u>: brain capillaries lack pores (fenestrae) and are bound by exceptionally tight junctions. This is known as the blood-brain barrier, which prevents access to water soluble chemicals, except those that can be actively transported. Reproductive cells, which have multiple layers separating them from capillaries, also restrict access to water soluble chemicals. Eggs (oocytes) are surrounded by granulosa cells and spermatogenic cells are surrounded by Sertoli cells which are tightly joined to form the blood-testis barrier. Transfer of water soluble chemicals is also restricted from crossing the placenta. Unfortunately, none of these barriers are effective against fat soluble chemicals, if they make it to these sites

3. <u>Distribution to storage sites</u>: some toxic chemicals accumulate in tissues which act as storage sites (fat is a great example) and the chemical does not exert significant toxic effects. When fat is lost quickly, the previously stored chemicals can be distributed and exert toxic effects, such as symptoms seen during fasting or rapid weight loss

4. <u>Association/Binding to Intracellular Binding proteins</u>: toxic chemicals can bind to and be trapped at non-target sites within the cell, which can temporarily reduce the amount of toxic chemical that is available to the target.

5. <u>Export from Cells</u>: toxic chemicals can be exported out of cells and back into the extracellular (between cells) space. The multidrug resistance (mdr) protein (or P-glycoprotein), will extract chemical(s) from the brain. The mdr contributes to the blood brain barrier. The female reproductive cells (oocytes) also have P-glycoprotein, which provide protection against toxic chemicals.

Metabolism (Biotransformation)

There are two phases of metabolism, which is also known as biotransformation – Phase I and Phase II. Overall, metabolism is the process of changing the toxin or toxicant into something that is able to be eliminated from the body. Metabolism or biotransformation is the primary mechanism for maintaining homeostasis during exposure to toxicants. The metabolism process can involve making a chemical that is highly fat-soluble into something that is water-soluble so that it can be eliminated in bile or urine.

Phase I Metabolism
During this phase a group of broad spectrum enzymes that are involved in hydrolysis (making the toxicant more water soluble), reduction (removing oxygen or reducing a functional group of the chemical to make it less toxic) and oxidation (adding oxygen to make the toxicant less toxic). The Phase I enzymes reactions expose or introduce a functional group [-OH (hydroxyl), $-NH_2$ (amine/amino), -SH (sulfhydryl) or -COOH (carboxyl)]. This phase usually results in only a slight increase in water solubility (hydrophilicity). The functional groups that are added or exposed during phase I metabolism are often the sites of phase II metabolism. Among the phase I biotransforming enzymes, the cytochrome P450 (cyp450) family are the leading group of enzymes. Cyp450 enzymes are referred to as a superfamily of enzymes. This importance is in regards to how many toxins and toxicants that the cyp450 family of enzymes can detoxify or activate to produce reactive by-products or intermediates. The cyp450 enzymes that are involved in metabolism of toxicants are found in greatest concentration in the liver, with the highest concentrations in the endoplasmic reticulum of the liver cells; cyp450 enzymes can be found to a lesser extent in practically all of the bodies' tissues.

Chapter 4: Mechanisms of Toxicity

<u>Phase II Metabolism</u>

The majority of phase II reactions will make the toxin or toxicant much more water soluble and will generally promote the excretion of the chemical. Phase II metabolism) may or may not be preceded by phase I metabolism. The phase II metabolism reactions include glucoronidation (glucoronic acids used to detoxify), sulfonation (sulfate used to detoxify), acetylation (acetyl group used to detoxify), methylation (methyl group used to detoxify), conjugation with glutathione (detoxication with glutathione tripeptide) and conjugation with amino acids (detoxication with amino acids). Phase II metabolism reactions tend to occur at a much faster rate than phase I metabolism reactions.

Excretion

Excretion is the removal of foreign chemicals from the blood and their subsequent transport to the outside of the body (return to the external environment). Excretion is the physical mechanism for toxic elimination. Non-volatile (non-evaporating), toxins and toxicants are removed primarily by the kidneys. The rate of excretion is based upon the physical and chemical properties of the chemicals. The major excretory organs – the liver and kidney efficiently remove highly water soluble and ionized chemicals (such as acids or bases). Water soluble chemicals dissolve easily into the aqueous urine and bile and fat soluble compounds are easily reabsorbed through cell to cell diffusion. For insecticides such as polychlorinated biphenyls (PCBs) and polyhalogenated bipheyls (PCHs), the body has no efficient removal systems, so elimination of these highly fat soluble, non-volatile species is very slow. These types of chemicals can be removed via excretion in mother's milk (dissolved in milk fats), excretion in bile and intestinal excretion; all of these processes are very inefficient. It goes without saying that the first mentioned elimination process, breastfeeding, exposes the offspring to these highly toxic chemicals upon consumption of mother's milk.

Reabsorption

Reabsorption of a toxic chemical not only delays its removal from the body, it also increases the amount of time specialized organs such as the kidney, gastrointestinal (GI) tract, are exposed to the toxicant. The longer the toxicant remains in the body the greater the chance it has to produce toxicity in one or more areas. Toxicants that make it to the kidney can diffuse across the organ and increase its concentration and residence time (duration) in the kidney by decreasing urine flow. When urine flow is slowed, the chemical remains in the kidney for a longer period of time. The process of diffusion reabsorption will depend upon how fat soluble the toxic chemical is. Diffusion of toxics such as acids or bases is dependent upon the pH of the kidney's tubular fluid. Metal reabsorption in the kidney is influenced by various transporters (recall the specialized transport systems in the distribution section). In the gastrointestinal (GI) tract toxicants can be reabsorbed by diffusion across intestinal mucosa. The toxicants' reabsorption in the GI tract occurs if they are highly fat soluble or are converted into more fat soluble forms while in the GI tract.

Toxication of a Chemical

Some toxins and toxicants are directly toxic and do not require a chemical reaction or metabolism into another toxic species. However, many chemicals undergo toxication or metabolic activation which converts (biotransformation) the original chemical into something that is harmful.

Classifications of Disease causing Toxins and Toxicants

You may have heard of certain chemicals being classified by words such as carcinogenic, mutagenic, teratogenic, etc., but do you know what these classifications mean? Here we will cover a few of the commonly used terms for classifying the type of toxicity or pathogenicity of certain chemicals so that you can understand their significance.

Carcinogens

Toxic chemicals or exposures that lead to the development of cancer are deemed carcinogens. Carcinogens can alter DNA permanently or they can cause other toxic effects such as speeding up cell division, which may increase the likelihood that genetic alterations (changes) or damage will occur. The potential for a carcinogen to cause cancer is based upon its degree of toxicity and the duration and dosage of exposure. Even if you are exposed to a carcinogen, you may not develop cancer. Each individual has unique genetic factors which influences cancer development. Lifestyle choices (nutrition, exercise, stress, living and working environment) also factors into whether or not cancer will develop. There are several agencies around the world that are dedicated to investigating causes of cancer. There are also a number of classification systems that allow the general public and professionals to recognize the cancer-causing potential of many toxins and toxicants.

The International Agency for Research on Cancer

The International Agency for Research on Cancer (IARC) is a part of the World Health Organization (WHO). The IARC carcinogen classification system is the most recognized and widely used. They have evaluated more than 900 chemical candidates and determined their potential to cause cancer. Only a little over 100 of the chemicals classified by IARC fall into the Class A – carcinogenic to humans category. These carcinogens are divided into the following IARC groups:

Group 1	Carcinogenic to humans
Group 2B	Possibly carcinogenic to humans
Group 2A	Probably carcinogenic to human
Group 3	Unclassifiable as to carcinogenicity in humans
Group 4	Probably not carcinogenic to humans

Source: World Health Organization

Environmental Protection Agency

The US Environmental Protection Agency (EPA) is a Federal agency which maintains an electronic database of known environmental contaminants and their health effects. This system is known as the Integrated Risk Information System (IRIS).

The EPA's rating system for carcinogens is very similar to IARC:

Group A	Carcinogenic to humans
Group B	Likely to be carcinogenic to humans
Group C	Suggestive evidence of carcinogenic potential
Group D	Inadequate information to assess carcinogenic potential
Group E	Not likely to be carcinogenic to humans

Source: EPA

National Toxicology Program

The National Toxicology Program (NTP) is a partnership of several different United States Federal agencies. NTP includes the National Institutes of Health (NIH), the Centers for Disease Control and Prevention (CDC), and the Food and Drug Administration (FDA). The NTP created its "Report on Carcinogens" (RoC) which lists over 200 chemicals and is periodically updated. The RoC does not list non-carcinogenic chemicals.

The NTP classifies carcinogens into 2 groups:

1. Known to be human carcinogens
2. Reasonably anticipated to be human carcinogens

Mutagens

Mutagens are toxins or toxicants that cause a change in genetic material. This usually refers to a change in DNA (deoxyribonucleic acid). Since mutations caused by mutagens often lead to cancer many mutagens are carcinogens as well. Mutagens act differently on DNA and can cause the changes in replication or transcription, by deleting or changing the genetic sequence. Mutagens can cause cell death or destruction of a particular gene or an accumulation of mutations that lead to cancerous tumor formation. Some examples of mutagens are ionizing radiation (alpha particles, gamma-rays, X-rays) or ultraviolet (UV) radiation or metals such as arsenic, cadmium or chromium.

Teratogens

A teratogen is a toxin or toxicant that can interfere with the development of an embryo or fetus. Teratogens can cause a birth defect or can end the pregnancy causing a miscarriage. Some examples of teratogens are alcohol, tobacco, caffeine, isotretinoin (acne medications – Retina-A, Accutane), blood thinners (warfarin – Coumadin).

Regulation of Toxics

There are several classes of regulations and many regulatory bodies around the world, as you just read in the carcinogens section of this chapter. When you see a regulatory limit do you know what all of the letters mean? And even if you can interpret the acronym does it make sense? Here we will cover commonly used regulatory language and agency names. These are commonly seen but not meant to be a comprehensive list.

Some widely known Regulatory Agencies or Groups:

ACGIH – America Conference of Governmental Industrial Hygienists (US)

CCOHS – Canada's National Centre for Occupational Health and Safety (Canada)

EPA – Environmental Protection Agency (US)

Chapter 4: Mechanisms of Toxicity

<u>FDA</u> – Food and Drug Administration (US)

<u>USDA</u> – United States Department of Agriculture (US)

<u>WHO</u> – World Health Organization (All countries who are members of the United Nations can have membership in WHO)

<u>Some commonly used Regulatory Acronyms</u>:

<u>IDLH</u> – Immediately Dangerous to Life or Health: This concentration is considered to be dangerous to life or may cause permanent toxic health effects. This value was originally used to determine whether or not a respirator needed to be used by workers.

<u>PEL</u> – Permissible Exposure Limit: This is the value or concentration of a toxicant that should not be exceeded (maximum value) over an 8 hour shift.

<u>REL</u> – Recommended Exposure limit: this is a recommended value (concentration) that should not be exceeded. Not binding by law.

<u>Air Regulations</u>
For air quality, the quantity is expressed in terms of the concentration of the contaminant in the atmosphere. The limit could refer to a maximum that should not be exceeded or a level that is averaged out over a set time period; in other words, you could exceed the limit for a short period of time, as long as the average concentration is under the limit.

<u>TWA</u> – Time Weighted Average: average concentration of a toxic chemical over a specified time period (such as 8 or 24 hours).

<u>TLV</u> – Threshold Limit Value: at or below this concentration toxicity should not be experienced by exposed persons.

TLV-C – Threshold Limit Value-ceiling: concentration that should not be exceeded during any part of the work period.

TLV-STEL – Threshold Limit Value – Short Term Exposure Limit: The concentration at which workers are not expected to experience toxic effects including irritation, chronic or irreversible damage, impaired judgment or decrement in work performance for a specified period of time (example 15 or 30 minutes), this limit also cannot cause exceedance of the TLV-TWA.

TLV-TWA – Threshold Limit Value – Time Weighted Average: The average, time-weighted concentration over a 8 hour workday and 40 hour workweek that workers can be exposed to daily without toxic effects.

TTC – Threshold of Toxicological Concern: Below this value there should be no considerable risk to human health for exposure to a group of chemicals.

Water Regulations
Water regulations generally specify the type of water that they are referring to. Most often, regulations that are seen are regarding drinking water. However natural bodies of water also have regulation values in order to limit the amount of toxic contamination.

MCL – Maximum Contaminant Level: the amount that should not be exceeded. The MCL may apply to drinking water, bodies of water and underground storage tanks that could leach into groundwater.

TDI – Tolerable Daily Intake: the estimated amount of a potentially toxic substance that can be ingested in water or food over a lifetime without any appreciable health risk.

TWI – Tolerable Weekly Intake: the estimated amount of a potentially toxic substance in drinking water or food that can be ingested weekly over a lifetime without appreciable health risk.

PWTI – Provisionally Tolerable Weekly Intake: a temporarily allowable intake of substances that cannot be avoided.

Chapter Summary

It is important to understand how toxins and toxicants can affect the health of people and our environment. It is just as important to know the mechanisms that we have in place once toxins and toxicants enter our bodies. If you know and understand the features of your car, then why shouldn't you know and understand the features of your body (More in Chapter 6)? Avoiding toxicity is not possible on this planet. The culture of the global society includes thousands of toxins and toxicants that are released into our air, water and soil. By assessing risk, we can become proactive in regards to controlling toxins and toxicants. Regulations are put into place, so that toxic chemicals can be monitored and controlled to minimize further damage to our health and environment. While this is a noble effort, it is by no means perfect.

5 Common Environmental Exposures

There are so many types and categories of environmental toxins and toxicants that we are exposed to – so many in fact that I could fill up many books if I were to list them all. However, there are broad categories that all of us should be aware of since they are common environmental contaminants. Because we are always in some type of environment, I feel that everyone should be somewhat aware of what we are exposing ourselves to outdoors and indoors. Since the chemical mixture in our environment is not consistent and is constantly changing, there is no way to always know what your exact exposure is. Since this is not a comprehensive list of all environmental contaminants, you may not see your "favorite" toxin or toxicant in this chapter, but stay tuned, I just might cover it in a future book.

Toxins

I. Fungus, Molds, Mildews

Many people are aware of or are becoming more conscious of the dangers of exposures to high mold concentrations in the air. Molds contain various types of mycotoxins; these are the toxic compounds that are emitted from many types of molds. However, molds are also an irritant structurally. They have hair-like projections called **hyphae**, which can cause severe allergy or allergenic-like symptoms. Therefore even molds that are considered nonpathogenic are still a potential health hazard since the allergenic symptoms can be severe.

Airborne mold spores are a combination of living and dead spores. Both the living and the dead spores can cause adverse health effects. Testing is the only way to determine the types of molds that are found in your home and the amount of living versus dead mold spores. It is key to remember that the test is a snapshot of what was present at the time of testing and that levels will vary as airflow is dynamic, moving and changing. If mold spores are small enough and penetrate into the lower airways and the body's defenses are unable to effectively isolate or remove them, toxicity will ensue.

Every year millions are exposed to excessive concentrations of molds that cause mild, moderate and severe health effects. It is not only important but critical to understand that we are all exposed to mold in our air on a **constant basis**. This is because mold spores are ubiquitous, which means that they are everywhere! Normally these toxins are at low enough concentrations that they do not bother or harm us. However, when their concentrations reach the point of toxicity, adverse health effects occur (or bad things happen). The dosage that is toxic often varies by individual (inter-individual variability is the term used by toxicologists). Therefore, when one family lives in a home, you may see severe symptoms in one family member and mild to no symptoms in other family members. Mold spore concentrations tend to elevate in areas of high moisture and/or humidity. Indoors, these tend to be areas of active leaks or may follow some type of water damage. Many of the newer household materials, such as sheetrock, are mold friendly.

Molds thrive on sheetrock when it is wet. If water damage occurs behind a wall with a vapor barrier, such as wallpaper, molds can concentrate and grow behind this material for years, creating a chronic exposure to the elevated levels of mold spores that are visually trapped behind the wall paper. Mold remediation (clean up and removal) became a big business in the 2000's; several people filed insurance claims for mold damage and non-qualified companies were created that claimed that they could appropriately remove mold contamination. Improper remediation of mold contamination can led to toxicity in the health of building occupants. Mold spores are invisible to the naked eye and can remain growing and providing toxic exposures to residents in areas if sheetrock is cut out in patches or people use bleach and paint to cover up past damage. In homes or buildings using soft, lined ductwork, the mold spores can also concentrate in this moist and often humid environment in the duct and increase in airborne concentrations, thereby introducing elevated doses into the home every time air passes across these surfaces and is shuttled into the air of your building's work or living space. Most buildings have hard unlined ductwork, most homes have soft, flexible lined ductwork.

II. Bacteria and Viruses

This is another section that can fill books! There are so many different bacteria and viruses that can cause toxicity. Exposures to these toxins can occur from many sources in the environment such as airborne, waterborne or foodborne. This section covers some of the major bacterial and viral toxins.

Bacterial Toxins

Bacterial protein toxins are the most powerful human poisons known. Even when they are highly diluted, they are still very potent. Food poisoning is the most common toxic effect of bacterial toxins. Symptoms from food poisoning can consist of diarrhea, stomach cramps, vomiting and will occur anywhere from 4-36 hours after consuming the contaminated food. Every year, it is estimated that numbers approaching

Chapter 5: Common Environmental Exposures

100 million people around the world suffer from food poisoning. It is difficult to determine the exact numbers as many cases that are moderate or severe are never reported.

Some common bacterial toxins from food poisoning include:

⅄ ***Clostridium botulinum* or Botulism**: *C. botulinum* toxins are some of the most deadly neurotoxins known to man. There are seven types (A-G) of botulinum toxins that cause muscle paralysis (types A, B, E and rarely F cause paralysis in humans). There are 3 types of botulism (1) foodborne botulism (2) infant botulism and (3) wound botulism. Botulism is a paralyzing muscle disease caused by *C. botulinum*. Symptoms from *C. botulinum* can include weakness, blurred vision, sensitivity to light, double vision, drooping eyelids, paralyzed eye nerves, difficulty speaking and swallowing, paralysis that spreads downward, respiratory failure and death. Wound botulism occurs when the neurotoxin is produced in a wound contaminated with *C. botulinum*. Generally symptoms from foodborne botulism occur within 6 hours - 10 days after consuming food contaminated with *C. botulinum*. Foodborne botulism is considered a public health emergency since other people may consume the contaminated food. Infant botulism can occur in a small number of susceptible infants that have *C. botulinum* in their intestinal tract. Botulism is not spread from person to person. Botulinum toxins have also been used to treat Strabismus (lazy eye deviation), facial spasms and blepharospasm (forced blinking and involuntary closing of the eye) in young patients. The FDA approved Botox to treat these ocular and facial conditions in 1989. In 2002 and more recently, the FDA approved

Botox to treat other common conditions such as skin wrinkles, underarm sweating, muscle pain disorders.

⅄ ***Salmonella*** **and** ***Shigella*** **(Shiga Toxin)**: *Salmonella* and *Shigella* are a group of bacterial species. These toxins will lead to fever, chills, bloody diarrhea and death in severe cases. Raw foods contaminated with these toxins are usually animal based (beef, poultry, eggs, milk), however, all foods, including vegetables, may become contaminated. Runoff water contaminated with fecal material from animal species can contaminate crops with these toxins. Thorough cooking will kill these bacterial toxins. Handling reptiles such as turtles and iguanas can also be a source of *Salmonella* contamination. People can be infected with Shigellosis, an infectious disease caused by *Shigella*. People contaminated by *Shigella* may or may not develop symptoms, even though they can transmit the toxin from person to person. Generally any symptoms from *Shigella* will resolve within 5-7 days. In children less than 2 years of age a severe *Shigella* infection can lead to high fever and seizures.

⅄ ***Escherichia coli***: *E. coli* sufferers will develop hemorrhagic colitis (very bloody diarrhea with very little stool), that can occur up to 3 days after initial food consumption. There are hundreds of strains of *E. coli* and some are typically found in the intestines of people and are harmless. However, when this powerful toxin causes infection, the severe symptoms previously mentioned can occur. Most often *E. coli* contamination is found in beef, generally during slaughter, and then mixed into ground beef – which looks and smells the same as non-contaminated beef. *E. coli* can also be transferred through drinking raw milk and unpasteurized juices. Swimming in or drinking contaminated waters are also a source of contamination. Vegetables have become infected by runoff from farms containing *Shiga* toxin producing *E. coli* (STEC) contamination. The runoff water affects soil and the crops grown in these contaminated soils. Transmission of the bacteria can also occur by caring for an individual that has an *E. coli* infection.

⅄ ***Listeria*** is a bacterium that causes a serious infection called listeriosis. Symptoms include muscle aches, fever and less commonly diarrhea. If the infection spreads to the central nervous system, symptoms can include the loss of balance, headache, stiff neck, confusion, and convulsions. It can also lead to meningitis or brain infection for a patient with a weakened immune system. *Listeria* bacteria are most commonly found in raw foods. Vegetables can be contaminated by soil and water carrying bacteria. *Listeria* is also found in raw animal products, such as meat and cheese. Babies can be born with listeriosis – if the mother consumes contaminated food during pregnancy, or worse, the infant can be miscarried or stillborn. The death rate among newborns with *Listeria* is 25–50%. According to the CDC approximately 300 deaths from *Listeria* occur annually.

Some other deadly bacterial toxins include:

⅄ **Tetanus:** is a disease that is caused by *Clostridium tetani* and leads to lockjaw (Trismus). Tetanus is a frequently fatal acute disease of the nervous system. Tetanus impairs the neuromuscular junction, which is the area between the nerve and the muscle that it is responsible for stimulation (impairment will lead to muscle spasms or a continuous contraction) and message transmission. This potent neurotoxin can enter the body through any puncture wound including nails, splinters, bites, burns, skin breaks and drug injections. Adults and children are advised to be immunized against Tetanus and a booster shot is recommended every ten years. *C. tetani* is found around the world in soil and in human and animal intestines. In infants tetanus can lead to spasms, the inability to nurse, and seizures.

⊿ **Pneumonia**: Pneumonia is a condition in which the alveoli of the lung become infected. The alveoli contain the lungs' defenders against toxics – the macrophages. Pneumonia is generally caused by an infection of the *Streptococcus* or *Mycoplasma* bacterial toxins. These bacteria can reside within the body for years without causing symptoms. Streptococcal pneumonia is the most common and is a more severe form of pneumonia. There are other rare forms of pneumonia that have been classified.

Viral Toxins

There are several viral toxins that affect human health every year. These viral toxins and their mechanisms are not easily defined. There are some general commonalities among these toxins such as (1) the ability to enter a host cell, (2) grow within the cell, (3) overtake the cells defense mechanisms and (4) cause temporary or permanent damage.

Viruses that are of concern due to their prevalence and toxic effects include the following:

Chapter 5: Common Environmental Exposures

⋏ **Rotavirus**: Rotavirus is the most common cause of severe diarrhea among children. The highest rates of illness occur among infants and young children and most children in the United States are infected by the rotavirus by the age of two. Adults infected with rotavirus generally show mild symptoms. It has been estimated that approximately 600,000 children die annually (worldwide) from rotavirus. The symptoms will generally appear after 2 days and include watery diarrhea and vomiting that lasts for 3-8 days along with abdominal pain and fever. Generally repeat rotavirus infections tend to be less severe than the original rotavirus infection. Rotavirus can be spread by accidental consumption of contaminated foods, touching contaminated surfaces and areas around toilets and diapers (non-waterproof covered diapers).

⋏ **Influenza Virus**: Influenza is caused by more than one virus. The virus attacks the respiratory tract and causes symptoms of fever, body aches, fatigue, coughing, sore throat, headaches and nasal congestion. In the US, it is estimated that 20,000 people die annually from the influenza virus. The virus is airborne and can be easily transmitted from person to person. The influenza viruses do not produce a toxin, but does cause toxic effects.

⋏ **Herpes Virus**: There are 8 types of herpes viruses – we will discuss the first four in this book. These viruses are not toxin producing viruses, but they do cause toxicity to various parts of the body and can even be carcinogenic.

Chapter 5: Common Environmental Exposures

1. <u>Human herpes simplex virus 1 (HSV 1)</u> causes cold sores (herpes labialis) most commonly. HSV 1 can also cause cutaneous herpes (skin herpes), genital herpes, gingivostomatitis (painful ulcers in the mouth), herpes encephalitis (brain inflammation), and keratoconjunctivitis (inflammation of the conjuctiva of the eye or cornea). HSV 1 is transmitted through physical contact.

2. <u>Human herpes simplex virus 2 (HSV 2)</u> can cause the same symptoms as HSV 1, but it most commonly causes genital herpes. HSV 2 is very common, 1 in 5 women have HSV 2 and they can transmit the virus to newborn babies. HSV 2 can lead to blindness of the newborn and also can affect the face, skin, mouth and internal organs. HSV 2 is transmitted through physical contact.

3. <u>Varicella-zoster (HHV-3 or VZV)</u> is the virus that causes chickenpox and shingles (herpes zoster). Chickenpox causes fever along with fluid-filled blisters that itch. Chickenpox is normally a childhood disease, but adults who do not contract it as a child can develop it. VZV is highly contagious and lasts about 7 days before symptoms disappear. The VZV will lie dormant in the ganglion nerves, and reactivate later in life as shingles which are wedge-shaped painful lesions on the skin.

4. <u>Epstein-Barr virus (EBV or HHV 4)</u> causes infectious mononucleosis (mono). Mono is passed through saliva, and is commonly transmitted by kissing. However, those sharing cups, glasses or eating utensils can pass EBV. Symptoms include sore throat, swollen lymph nodes and prolonged fatigue. EBV can cause the spleen to swell, making it susceptible to

rupture. EBV can rarely cause some forms of cancer, including nasopharyngeal carcinoma (nose and throat cancer) and Hodgkin's lymphoma (lymphatic system cancer)

⋏ **Human Immunodeficiency Virus (HIV) / Acquired Immune Deficiency Syndrome (AIDS)**: HIV is a group of viruses called the retroviruses. HIV causes AIDS, and this disease typically progresses 10 years after initially being infected with HIV. When AIDS develops the immune system is so damaged that the person is susceptible to a number of opportunistic infections that would not affect a person with a normal immune system. Symptoms vary based upon the phase of the infection. The HIV virus may be passed from person to person when a non-infected person's broken skin or mucous membranes come in contact with infected blood, semen, or vaginal secretions. HIV can be passed through breastfeeding and in-utero.

Toxicants

I. Solvents

The majority of solvents become a part of the environment by evaporating into the atmosphere. Solvents are liquid chemicals that have varying degrees of fat and water solubility. They also differ in volatility, charge and molecular size. Solvents are easily absorbed across the skin, lung and gastrointestinal tract. There are a number of classes of solvents; we will discuss some solvent classes and some distinct solvents of interest (due to their frequency or severity) in separate sections.

Solvent classes include:

Chapter 5: Common Environmental Exposures

- aliphatic hydrocarbons
- chlorinated hydrocarbons
- aromatic hydrocarbons
- alcohols
- ethers
- esters and acetates
- amides and amines
- aldehydes
- ketones
- other complex mixtures that are unclassified

Solvents tend to increase in fat solubility as the molecular weight of the chemicals that are contained in the solvent increases. Solvents are used commonly in the home. Solvents are used to dissolve, disperse and dilute materials that are not water-soluble. Most solvents are petroleum products that have been refined into a particular type of solvent. The majority of solvents also produce some degree of depression or damage (which can be reversible and/or irreversible) to the central nervous system.

People are exposed to solvents on a daily basis during normal activities. In other words, you do not have to go out of your way to be exposed to solvents. Solvents are found in our air and water because of normal human activities. When solvents contaminate groundwater, this water can end up in households. Once in our homes, the water can be introduced into the body through multiple routes (inhalation, dermal absorption and oral ingestion/absorption). Recall that solvents are easily absorbed through the skin, lung and GI tract, which are all accessible through one or more of these multiple routes of exposure.

Most often, people are generally exposed to low-levels of solvents that are mixtures of multiple types of solvents as opposed to single compounds. High concentrations of solvents are also rare; however, incidences like these can occur when accidental releases take place. Your exposure also will depend upon the area that you live and work in and/or your occupational exposure.

Toxicologists and other professionals have had much scientific debate over how these long-term exposures result in neurological disorders. Some examples are *organic solvent syndrome, psychoorganic syndrome, painter's syndrome* and *chronic solvent encephalopathy* (CSE). CSE has a broad spectrum of symptoms including fatigue, headache, sleep disorders, that may or may not have accompanying changes in neurophysiological function. Many people have these "non-specific" symptoms and may not be aware that they have CSE. When no neurophysiological changes are noted, but symptoms are experienced, Neuroasthetic syndrome is diagnosed, which is a reversible form of CSE. More severe or even moderate forms of CSE will cause some neurophysiological changes that may or may not be reversible. Again, there is much debate on both sides about the effects of chronic exposures to solvents. More objective research studies in this area are needed to provide evidence of how chronic low-level exposures to solvents affect human health long-term and the varying degrees of toxicity.

Solvents in the Environment

Solvents enter the atmosphere primarily through evaporation. They are also released through industrial production, processing and transport, amongst others. Most solvents are lightweight volatile organic compounds (VOCs). These solvents evaporate after use, such as while they are drying (cleaning products, aerosols, fumigators, paints, paint thinners) or when exposed during use (gasoline, naphtha, propellants).

Solvents concentrate in the atmosphere and are carried around the globe through winds. These winds will disperse solvents to far reaching areas (hundreds or thousands of miles from the location of the initial release).

Wind also dilutes the concentration of solvents in the atmosphere, which is why concentrations of VOCs in the air are generally low. This type of contamination will vary depending upon the area. This variation is also part of the reason that air quality is regularly monitored for VOC contaminants (along with other airborne contaminants) in highly industrial areas or highly populous urban areas.

VOCs can also enter into the ground water since they are all water-soluble to some extent. When a VOC spill occurs, the majority will evaporate into the air, that portion that does enter the soil (VOCs will pass through the soil and migrate to underlying insoluble material or water – whichever is underneath) and ground water will either concentrate at the surface (surface water contamination) or sink to the bottom of the water. A considerable percentage of the VOCs will evaporate (surface contaminants) from these waters and enter the atmosphere while a portion may adversely affect the species that live in these bodies of water. VOCs that reach the bottom may eventually migrate back up to the surface, through currents or waves mixing the waters to reach the surface, or by slowly dissolving in the water. Bottom contaminants usually remain there until they are brought to the surface by water mixing. The density of the VOC will dictate whether or not it will settle at the surface or the bottom of groundwater. Regulatory Toxicologists set limits for these types of contaminants that end up in air and water. These regulated limits will vary from country to country and at times even state to state in the US. The risk assessment that is conducted by these toxicologists is meant to protect the most vulnerable types of citizens in the environment.

Formaldehyde

General Characteristics
Formaldehyde is a colorless gas or liquid with a strong scent. It is also known as formalin and methyl aldehyde. Formaldehyde is used in a

variety of products such as disinfectants, fungicides, adhesives, cosmetics, deodorant, detergents, dyes, fertilizer, foam insulation, synthetic lubricants, paints, plastic, rubber, textile, resins, garden hardware, and water softeners. Formaldehyde has such a wide reach in our everyday lives that it is difficult to avoid some form of exposure.

Formaldehyde Toxicity
Formaldehyde causes respiratory irritation, as well as being an irritant to the eyes, nose and throat. Formaldehyde can lead to upper respiratory tract irritation, coughing and bronchitis. Formaldehyde can cause asthma to develop and high concentrations can cause pneumonia. Formaldehyde can damage genetic material and damage DNA repair mechanisms. Formaldehyde is classified as a suspected human carcinogen. Formaldehyde toxicity is often misdiagnosed as having asthma, bronchitis, anxiety, depression or hypochondria (belief that symptoms are serious when there is no medical evidence to support it). Infant exposure to chronic levels of formaldehyde gas vapors can lead to severe and prolonged diarrhea and vomiting. People can become chemically sensitized to formaldehyde.

Formaldehyde in the environment
Formaldehyde is found in the household materials that we mentioned in the general characteristics section. Formaldehyde offgases (evaporates) from sealants and other materials such as particleboard, insulation and plywood. Formaldehyde is also used as a tissue fixative and for embalming.

Formaldehyde Regulations
The NTP has classified formaldehyde as known to be a human carcinogen. On July 7, 2010, the US established a law, the Formaldehyde Standards for Composite Wood Products Act, which directs the EPA to come up with regulations to be implemented by January 1, 2013. California currently has limits set for formaldehyde in composite wood

products for particleboard at 0.09 ppm, medium density fiberboard at 0.11 ppm. Several European countries have set regulations for formaldehyde under E1 and E2 emissions classification for uncoated particleboard/OSB/MDF <8g/100g dry board; for uncoated hardwood plywood, solid wood panels and coated particleboard at <0.13 mg/m^3/hour.

II. Hydrocarbons

Gasolines are complex solvents that contain hundreds of chemical compounds. Differences in chemical structures, even slight ones, can dramatically change the toxicity. While many of us are exposed to gasoline routinely throughout our lives, there are a number of other hydrocarbons that we are often exposed to but often may not consider. These toxic agents are of great interest to Environmental Toxicologists due to their prevalence and effect on the environment.

Aromatic Hydrocarbons

Hydrocarbons are chemicals that consist entirely of both Hydrogen and Carbon atoms in their structure. Aromatic is the distinct aroma (generally sweet-smelling) that these toxic chemicals possess.

Benzene

General Characteristics
Benzene is a ring-shaped aromatic hydrocarbon that is used to synthesize (make) other chemicals and is a major components of gasoline (as an anti-knocking agent). Benzene was first isolated from coal tar but is now made primarily from petroleum products. Benzene has a sweet odor (hence the term aromatic) and is formed through incomplete combustion of organic compounds. Benzene is also used for the synthesis of dyes, lubricants, detergents, drugs, certain types of rubbers and pesticides. Benzene (at room temperature) is a colorless or yellow liquid. Benzene

can be formed by natural or man-made processes. Some natural sources of benzene are volcanoes and forest fires. Benzene is also found naturally in crude oil, gasoline, and cigarette smoke. Benzene evaporates rapidly in the air and since it is heavier than air, it can settle into low lying places. Benzene is one of the top 20 chemicals produced in the United States.

Environmental Exposure to Benzene
Environmentally, there are several routes of exposure to Benzene. Benzene is released in the environment primarily through emission of gasoline vapors and automobile exhaust. In outdoor air, low concentrations of benzene are also created by tobacco smoke, gasoline stations, and industrial emissions. The highest contributor of benzene to environmental contamination is through industrial processes. Emissions from coal and oil, burning benzene waste, storage, evaporation from gasoline service stations, and the use of industrial benzene-containing solvents are more examples of environmental contamination. Benzene can also contaminate the environment's water and soil through industrial discharge, disposal of benzene containing products, and leaking gasoline from underground storage tanks – benzene can leach (leak) from Underground Storage Tanks (UST) or Petroleum Storage Tanks (PST) and from hazardous waste sites that have benzene-containing well water.

Indoor Exposure to Benzene
Indoor air generally has higher concentrations of benzene than does outdoor air. Benzene contamination of the air indoors comes from multiple sources such as adhesives/glues, detergents, furniture wax, and paint. Air quality near gasoline stations and hazardous waste sites has higher concentrations of benzene than does other areas, and can contribute to the indoor air concentrations in homes and buildings situated around these areas – via air exchanges from Heating Ventilation and Cooling Systems (HVAC).

In regards to personal exposure at work, people who work in industries that use or produce benzene are generally exposed to the highest concentrations. Tobacco is another major source of benzene for the general public. The release of benzene from cigarette smoke contributes to the elevated (6-10 times higher) body burdens that are tolerated by smokers. Inside your car, offgassing (evaporation) of adhesives and products used to clean the vehicle can contribute to benzene contamination. However, in vehicles the primary source of benzene exposure will be via air exchange through your ventilation system if you routinely sit in traffic.

Benzene Toxicity

Benzene causes toxicity by stopping your cells from functioning properly. Examples include damage to the immune system and insufficient production of red blood cells. Benzene and its metabolites (chemical by-products) can be highly toxic in the body. Benzene is a suspected carcinogen (cancer causing). Benzene is toxic to blood (hematopoietic) and long-term exposure may initially cause anemia (low blood cell count/low hemoglobin), leukopenia (white blood cell decrease – the disease and infection fighting cells) or thrombopenia / thrombocytopenia (decrease in blood platelets – platelets are important for blood clotting) or a combination of these disorders. Benzene can also cause bone marrow depression; the degree of this depression is dependent upon the dosage.

As benzene exposures continue, diseases can develop that are often fatal such as pancytopenia (also known as aplastic anemia a condition in which there is a decrease in all 3 types of blood cells – red, white and platelets, and which causes bone marrow lose the ability to produce sufficient amounts of new cells to replenish blood cells) and marrow aplasia (reduction of stem cells in the bone marrow which reduces the ability to produce all types of blood cells).

If a person contracts these diseases and does survive they will often suffer from myelodisplasia (a group of blood disorders associated with bone marrow malfunction) which is also termed pre-leukemia since this disease will often progress to <u>myelogenous leukemia</u>. Myelogenous leukemia is a cancer that can either be classified as acute myelogenous leukemia (AML) or chronic myelogenous leukemia (CML). CML is an uncommon type of cancer of the blood cells. "Chronic" in the disease name "chronic myelogenous leukemia" does not refer to the length of exposure but rather that this cancer tends to progress more slowly than AML. The word "acute" in the disease name "acute myelogenous leukemia" describes its rapid progression. The word "myelogenous" refers to the disease's effect on white blood cells (myeloid cells). Myeloid cells are those cells that mature into the various types blood cells, including red and white blood cells and platelets.

<u>Benzene Regulation</u>

Due to the widespread use and production of benzene and the severity of its toxicity, there are varying strict limits for benzene exposure in the environment. For workers in the US, the Occupational Safety & Health Administration (OSHA) set a permissible exposure limit (PEL) for benzene exposure at 1 ppm Time-Weighted Average (TWA) over an 8-hr workday and no greater than 5 ppm for 15 minutes in a work period. The National Institute of Occupational Safety & Health (NIOSH) has a recommended exposure limit (REL) for benzene set at 0.1 ppm TWA over a 10 hour workday and no greater than 1 ppm short-term exposure limit (STEL) during a 15 minute work period. NIOSH considers benzene to be immediately dangerous to life and health (IDLH) at an airborne concentration of 500 ppm. The American Conference of Governmental Industrial Hygienists (ACGIH) and Canadian Centre for Occupational Health Exposure (CCOHS) set PELs for benzene exposure at 0.5 ppm TWA over an 8 hour workday and no greater than 2.5 ppm for a STEL.

Toluene

<u>General Characteristics</u>

Chapter 5: Common Environmental Exposures

Toluene is another aromatic hydrocarbon. Toluene is a colorless and clear liquid and has a distinct aromatic scent. Toluene occurs naturally in the Tolu Tree and in crude oil. Toluene is produced by gasoline and other fuel production as well. Toluene is used to make paints, paint thinners, fingernail polish, adhesives, lacquers, shoe polish (think back to your home list of products containing toxic ingredients) rubber, in some printing processes and leather tanning. Toluene is also referred to as methylbenzene, toluol, and phenylmethane.

Environmental Exposure to Toluene
Like benzene, toluene enters the environment through the use of products containing toluene. It is also a gasoline additive, which has increased over the years contributing to even more toluene in the environment. Toluene is readily broken down to other chemicals by microorganisms found in soil and evaporates from surface waters and surface soils; therefore it is removed from the environment relatively quickly. If toluene is in underground well water, where microorganisms are not available to break it down, it will remain for a longer period, until it is brought to the surface to evaporate into the air.

Toluene Toxicity
Toluene is not a carcinogen, but it is a volatile organic compound that can affect the central nervous system (CNS) and cardiovascular system (CV). Occupational asthma has occurred in some workers routinely exposed to toluene. Toxicity from toluene can also occur from the inhalation of fumes (either accidentally or intentionally), ingestion, or dermal (skin) absorption. Glue sniffing or the intentional abuse of toluene containing adhesives is a widespread issue and has been found to be most problematic among children and teens due to its low cost and ease of accessibility around the home and in retail stores. Toluene abuse has been frequently documented by saturation of cloth with spray paint which is then placed over the nose and mouth for inhalation, CNS toxicity will then occur and give the abuser a sensation of euphoria or high.

Bagging is the inhalation of spray paint in a bag and is another often documented form of toluene abuse. The abuser re-inhales the exhaled toluene and CO_2 fumes in the bag which can lead to disorientation, hypoxia (reduction of the supply or oxygen at levels needed to sustain tissue or life) and hypercarbia (abnormally high carbon dioxide in the blood).

Toluene Regulation
The US OSHA PEL for toluene is set at 200 ppm TWA/TWL over an 8 hour period) and at 300 ppm for no longer than 10 minutes, and is IDLH at 500 ppm. ACGIH TLV is 50 ppm. The NIOSH REL is 100 ppm TWA for 8 hours and 150 ppm STEL for 15 minutes. These are all airborne concentrations.

Xylenes

General Characteristics
Xylene is a set of three isomers (chemical compounds with the same molecular structure but different structural formulas) of dimethylbenzene. This is two methyl (CH_3) groups attached to a benzene ring. The three forms of xylene are ortho-Xylene (o-Xylene), meta-Xylene (m-Xylene) and para-Xylene (p-Xylene) and the names are based upon which part of the benzene ring that the methyl groups are attached to (this is the variation in structure which makes them isomers). Xylene is a clear and colorless liquid with an aromatic scent. Xylene is also known by the following names Dimethyl benzene, Xylol, Methyl toluene, 1, 4-dimethyl-benzene and Violet 3.

Xylene Environmental Exposure
Xylene is used industrially in gasoline (the amount varies from 0.5 – 1%). Xylene is generally used as a mixture of the three isomers with m-Xylene being the most predominant. The xylene mixture is primarily used as a

solvent in laboratories and in the chemical, petrochemical and medical industries.

<u>Xylene Toxicity</u>
Xylenes are considered low in toxicity since the majority of it is readily excreted or respired from the body unchanged. Xylene vapors are absorbed rapidly from the lungs and slowly through the skin (dermal). Xylene liquid is also absorbed slowly through dermal contact. The portion of Xylene that is absorbed is metabolized by the liver to methylhippuric acid (MHA). The majority of MHA (70-80%) is excreted in the urine and is a good biomarker to detect human for exposure to Xylene. At high concentrations xylene causes central nervous system effects such as psychological and physiological changes and malfunctions. Chronic exposure to xylene has been linked to anemia, and deficiencies of white blood cells (leukopenia) and thrombocytes (thrombocytopenia), chest pain, shortness of breath (dyspnea) and blue or purple skin discolorations (cyanosis) and respiratory symptoms.

<u>Xylene Regulation</u>
The US OSHA PEL for xylene is set at a concentration of 100 ppm over an 8-hour TWA. NIOSH RELs for xylene are 100 ppm as a TWA for up to a 10-hour shift period and a 40-hour workweek and at 200 ppm for 10 minutes STEL. The US ACGIH threshold limit value (TLV) for xylene is 100 ppm an 8-hour workday and a 40-hour workweek and a STEL of 150 ppm not to exceed 15 minutes. These are all airborne concentrations.

III. Chlorinated Hydrocarbons

Chlorinated hydrocarbons are hydrocarbons that have at least one Chlorine (Cl) atom attached to a Carbon (C) atom (also referred to as organochlorine chemistry). Chlorinated hydrocarbons are also known as chlorocarbons and organochlorines. Some chlorinated hydrocarbons are naturally formed, but the vast majority of them are man-made.

Organochlorine chemistry is used to make a wide variety of products and applications. We will discuss some common chlorinated hydrocarbons that we can be routinely exposed to.

Vinyl Chloride

General Information
Vinyl Chloride is colorless and has a sweet mild odor. It is slightly soluble in water and very flammable. The largest use of organochlorine chemistry is in the production of vinyl chloride. The majority of vinyl chloride is used to produce polyvinyl chloride (PVC). PVC is widely used because it is cheap, durable and easily formed into shapes needed such as piping, siding or fittings. The addition of plasticizers (a chemical added to plastics to increase their flexibility, transparency, durability and longevity), such as phthalate to soften PVC, expands its use to clothing and upholstery, inflatable products, electrical insulation and has replaced the use of rubber in many cases. PVC may have chemical differences, so the term polyvinyl chloride or PVC can be a generic catch-all for a class of synthetic plastics.

Phthalates (Plasticizer for PVC)
We cover phthalates here because it is commonly added to the PVC that we are exposed to. Phthalate is derived from phthalic acid (a benzene based acid which has 2 isomers isophthalic and terephthalic acid), which is considered low in toxicity. Phthalates are used widely (millions of tons annually) in enteric coatings (these coating barriers keep the pill intact until it reaches the small intestine) of pharmaceutical pills and nutritional supplements, lubricants, detergents, packaging, children's toys, modeling clay, paints , waxes, printing inks, textile, food products, personal care products (makeup, moisturizer, nail polish, liquid soap, hair products), medical devices, catheters, blood transfusion devices, caulk, adult toys, emulsifying agents, adhesives and glues, plastic furniture, plastic pools

and the list goes on. There are several types of phthalates. Bensylbutylphthalate (BBP) is used in manufacturing PVC.

Vinyl Chloride Toxicity

Vinyl Chloride is toxic to the central nervous system and can cause dizziness, fatigue, headaches and giddiness through acute exposure(s). Extremely high acute exposures have caused fainting, lung and kidney irritation, the inhibition of blood clotting in humans and cardiac arrhythmias in animals. Chronic exposure to vinyl chloride through oral ingestion and inhalation is toxic to the liver. The Environmental Protection Agency (EPA) has classified vinyl chloride as a carcinogen (cancer-causing).

Non-cancer toxicity includes Vinyl Chloride disease, which is a multi-system disorder that causes (1) blood spasms to fingers that become white due to a lack of blood flow and numbness and pain to the fingers is experienced upon exposure to the cold temperatures or strong emotions (Raynaud's phenomenon) (2) thrombocytopenia–thrombocyte deficiency, (3) liver and (4) lung dysfunction, (5) portal fibrosis (damage to the portal vein of the liver) and (6) acroosteolysis (ulcers on the palms of the hands and soles of the feet).

Reproductive and developmental toxicity caused by vinyl chloride includes evidence of male sexual performance being adversely affected. Other scientific evidence has shown the increase of birth defects in women exposed during pregnancy. Increased miscarriages in the wives of men exposed to vinyl chloride have also been demonstrated. Testicular damage and decreased male fertility was shown in rats exposed to vinyl chloride.

Thermal Decomposition of PVC

While PVC (made primarily from vinyl chloride) is considered to be the most flame resistant of polymers (natural and man-made), they are very toxic when they undergo pyrolysis (heated to form smoke) and burning.

PVC which is used so commonly that it can be considered a source of fuel during a home or building fire. The thermal combustion products and decomposition products from PVC pyrolysis causes adverse health effects and death to firefighters and building occupants. PVC has a number of additives besides plasticizers, such as catalysts, lubricants, heat and light stabilizers, fire and smoke retardants, reinforcing agents and fillers. The variation of these additives changes the composition of combustion and pyrolysis products as well as how fire resistant the PVC is. PVC releases hydrochloric acid (HCl) as it is heated. The hotter that the PVC becomes the greater the amount of HCl that is released, this leads to the breaking apart of the long-chain chemistry of the PVC polymer and the production of smoke particles, benzene (the most prevalent compound released), carbon dioxide (CO_2), carbon monoxide (CO) and approximately 70 other compounds which are produced and released as a result of the thermal breakdown of PVC.

Pulmonary damage occurs from the inhalation of PVC thermal breakdown products. The acute inhalation toxicity is attributed almost entirely to the presence of CO (asphyxiant) and HCl (lung respiration and lung sensory irritant). Hydrogen cyanide (HCN) is also a highly toxic breakdown product that can be liberated from PVC thermal breakdown. Chronic exposures to PVC thermal breakdown products are not well understood. Most persons exposed to PVC thermal breakdown products die if they are not quickly removed from the environment as low levels of these contaminants are highly toxic. Due to the large amount of chlorine contained in PVCs, the release of dioxin has been documented in the manufacture or burning of PVC.

Polychlorinated Biphenyls (PCBs)

<u>General Information</u>
PCBs are industrial pollutants. They are used as insulators for electricity and heat transfer agents. PCBs are complex chemical mixtures that can

vary in chemical composition (meaning there is more than one type of PCB). PCBs were banned in the US in 1979.

PCB Exposure

Even though PCBs were banned, they may be found in products manufactured before 1979, such as PCB capacitors, cable insulation, adhesives, tapes, electrical insulation, hydraulic systems and motors, caulking, oil-based paints, floor finishes, plastics, carbonless copy paper, transformers and capacitors and other electrical equipment. PCBs can leach out through poorly maintained hazardous landfills, leaking from electrical transformers and illegal dumping. PCBs are very persistent and do not easily break down in the environment. PCBs can cycle through the environment through air, water and soil. PCBs can accumulate in above ground leaves of plants and crops and can bioaccumulate in fish. PCBs can travel long distances and has been found in areas that are far from the original source.

PCB Toxicity

PCBs can cause toxicity to the immune system, reproductive system, nervous system, and endocrine system. The EPA has determined that PCBs are probable human carcinogens. The IARC has stated that PCBs are probably carcinogenic to humans. The NTP has said that it is reasonable to conclude that PCBs are carcinogenic in humans. NIOSH has concluded that PCBs are a potential occupational carcinogen.

IV. Asbestos

Asbestos is the name of a group of six different fibrous minerals – amosite, chrysotile, crocidolite and the fibrous form of the following minerals – tremolite, actinolite, and anthophyllite (the last 3 also have a non-asbestiform variety). All six forms of asbestos are found in the environment naturally. Asbestos is an inorganic (non-biological) toxicant.

Chapter 5: Common Environmental Exposures

Naturally occurring asbestos (NOA) can be found in certain rock formations. If the NOA remains undisturbed it does not pose a health threat. Weathering or human disturbance can easily break down NOA into airborne fibers. In 2005, the US Geological Survey (USGS) reported that there are 324 locations of NOA in the Eastern US. California has also conducted a study of NOA in El Dorado County, in an area where asbestos was found in soils near a high school.

Asbestos has been used to make other products that are toxic. Asbestos is a material that was used widely prior to the discovery of its toxicity. The asbestos mineral fiber was used as a fire-retardant and as insulation material. Due to the strength of the asbestos fiber and its flame resistance, it was also used in a wide range of manufactured items such as roofing shingles, tiles for ceilings and floors, paper products, cement products, automobile friction products for brake transmission and clutch parts, heat-resistant fabrics, coatings, gaskets and packaging.

The toxicity of asbestos largely lies in its fiber shape. These microscopic fibers become airborne when disturbed during demolition or damage. These airborne fibers can be inhaled into the lungs and are not easily isolated by the lungs. Macrophages (the lungs "clean-up crew" for isolating toxics) try to engulf asbestos fibers, but they are not easily engulfed and remain partially exposed causing chronic exposure and toxicity. Asbestos can lead to severe health problems including mesothelioma, which is a rare form of cancer attributed to asbestos exposure. Asbestos can be carried by water or wind for long distances. Asbestos is not easily broken down and will remain virtually unchanged in water and soil.

The use of asbestos-containing materials in new construction is prohibited in the US. Most asbestos-containing materials were banned by the EPA in 1989. This was overturned by the Fifth Circuit Court of Appeals in New Orleans in 1991. However, the following remained banned under the court's decision - flooring felt, rollboard, and corrugated, commercial, or specialty paper and new uses of asbestos. There are many sources of exposure due to the widespread use.

Vermiculite is a naturally occurring mineral composed of shiny flakes that resemble mica. Vermiculite flakes expand as much as 8-30 times their original size when heated and become a light-weight and fire-resistant material. Vermiculite has been used in many products, including wall and attic insulation. The majority of vermiculite sold (over 70%) in the US from 1919–1990 came from a mine that was contaminated with asbestos in Libby, Montana and was often sold as Zonolite (brand name of the vermiculite). If you have vermiculite insulation in your home, you should assume it is contaminated with asbestos.

Since the remediation or abatement of asbestos is very expensive, there are many buildings (particularly older construction) that have asbestos-containing materials in place. If asbestos is not disturbed it is not a hazard, which is why there are normally signs that warn people of asbestos containing materials in public places. It is important to be aware of any asbestos-containing materials in your home or living space, since damage could cause exposure to occupants.

IV. Mercury

General Characteristics: Mercury (Hg) is an elemental metal and is the only metal that is found as a liquid at normal temperatures. Mercury is found in the environment naturally and can also be introduced by man-made processes. Hg is a heavy liquid that is silvery-white in color. Hg forms metal alloys with gold, silver and other metals. These metal alloys are also called amalgams. Hg is also known as quicksilver and due to its high density it is used in barometers and thermometers. Hg is a poor conductor of heat compared to other metals. Hg conducts electricity fairly well and is used in some fluorescent lighting, batteries and in the manufacture of chlorine and sodium hydroxide. Calomel, a mercury compound, was used in the medical industry as a purgative, in laboratory electrodes for electrochemical measurements and as a fungicide.

Mercury Toxicity: Mercury (Hg) is a naturally occurring element that is highly toxic and whose effects can be widespread. There are many well documented cases of mercury's toxicity. Mercury concentrates in the muscle tissue of fish (not the fat or skin) so it cannot be easily removed or cooked out of the food. Its most toxic form is Methylmercury (MeHg). MeHg affects the immune system, the nervous system and is highly toxic to developing embryos. MeHg exposure is generally through ingestion; it is excreted much more slowly and absorbed much easier than other forms of mercury.

Hg (liquid elemental form) can cause tremors (shaking) and gingivitis. Chronic inhalation of Hg can lead to excitability. Elemental Hg that is ingested is absorbed slowly (compared to mercury compounds such as MeHg) and may pass through the digestive system without causing toxicity or damage. Mercury chloride salt is highly toxic to the gastrointestinal tract and will cause kidney failure. Mercury emissions can bioaccumulate in fish and wildlife which is consumed by people. Pregnant women are often cautioned to avoid fish due to possible mercury contamination and toxicity to their developing child.

Note: Bioaccumulation of chemicals and other contaminants can occur when a higher species consumes a lower species and retains that chemical contaminant of the lower species; as the consumption of the chemically contaminated species move higher up the food chain, the chemical can become greater in concentration and ultimately affect the health of humans. It is the process by which organisms can take-up toxins, toxicants and other contaminants faster than they can eliminate them, increasing their load over time. If the contamination is removed and sufficient time has passed, the load can decrease.

Chapter 5: Common Environmental Exposures

Environmental Exposure to Mercury: Mercury will become available in the environment due to normal breakdown of rocks and soil and is carried by wind and water. Hg can also be released into the air by volcanic eruption or, rarely, in some volcanic non-eruption emissions (gases, ash). Natural Hg release has been relatively stable over the years, but environmental concentrations of Hg are increasing (by estimates of 1.5% annually) due to man-made processes, such as fossil fuel combustion, mining, smelting and the combustion of solid waste. Fertilizers release Hg directly into soil (sometimes contaminating vegetables and other consumed crops) or water (contaminating fish). All Hg in the environment will ultimately end up in soil and surface waters. Cattle breeding products also contain mercury.

Mercury Regulations: The US is considered the top exporter of Hg. In 2008, the Mercury Export Ban Act took effect in the US. It has language regarding long-term management and storage of Hg and export controls. The act is meant to reduce the amount of Hg in the environment. It only bans elemental mercury, but does not cover mercury compounds. There are also opportunities to apply for a waiver to the export ban on elemental mercury. Most recently the EPA proposed a rule restricting the use of elemental mercury in barometers, manometers, and hygrometers/ psychrometers (measures humidity). The proposal would require persons to notify the EPA in advance of any manufacture, import, export or distribution of these products. The proposed "required notification" to the EPA would allow the agency to evaluate the intended use and, if necessary, to prohibit or limit the Hg activity before it occurs.

There are many regulatory limits that have been set worldwide and state by state in the US for mercury. Here we list a few key regulations which are concentrations that should not be exceeded when averaged out over a given time-period. The OSHA PEL for 8 hr TWA exposure is 0.1 mg/m^3. The EPA MCL for water is 0.002 mg/L and <0.25 µg/m^3 average over 24 hours. The WHO sets the drinking water limit to 0.001 mg/L (for all forms of mercury) and 5 μg/kg (micrograms per kilogram of air) total Hg and 3.3 μg/kg of MeHg for weekly airborne intake. The FDA Action Levels (ALs) in food and animal feed are 1 ppm and 0.002 μg/L in bottled water. The EPA also sets a limit for municipal solid waste landfills (MCLs) at 0.002 μg/L and at no more than 0.009 mg/L for a single composite sample of waste.

V. Pesticides

Many of the pesticides that I will discuss in this section are an issue in regards to toxic exposures. Several of them have been banned in the US for years. However, these pesticides are highly persistent, meaning that they are not easy to remove from our environment, since they do not breakdown quickly – many taking years or decades to breakdown. They also bioaccumulate and tend to be highly fat soluble, meaning that when you are exposed to them, they are stored in your fatty tissues. Removal of chemicals stored in fatty tissues is very inefficient in the human body and can remain stored in your body for many years. While not all pesticides will be included in this section, we will cover those that remain a top concern in regards to toxic exposures and adverse health effects.

DDT (Dichlorophenyl trichloroethane)
General Information

DDT is a pesticide, that has been banned in several countries for decades (banned in 1972 in the US) yet its presence is still found in our environment due to its persistence (slow elimination from the environment). Some parts of the world still use DDT for disease control (malaria) and agriculturally. DDT and it byproducts DDE and DDD are all toxic, persistent, bioaccumulative (accumulate up the biological food chain). DDT was first used in WWII as a pesticide and has been used to control pests in agriculture such as potatoes, corn, apples, cotton and tobacco.

Environmental Exposure to DDT

DDT in soil can be absorbed by growing plants and the consumption of these foods. DDT is absorbed by fish and shellfish that are in contaminated water and we are exposed by eating them in prepared food. DDT can also be transferred to babies through breastfeeding. DDT is found in various soils and in sediment runoff and is deposited in our atmosphere. DDT can take 15 years or more to break down in the environment. The consumption of fish in contaminated waters is documented in many waterways including the Great Lakes ecosystem in the US.

DDT Toxicity
DDT causes damage to the liver (and can lead to the development of liver cancer). DDT is classified as a probable human carcinogen. DDT causes temporary damage to the nervous system and the reproductive system. DDT is genotoxic (toxic to DNA) and is an endocrine disruptor (hormone system toxicity). DDT and DDE have been linked to the development of diabetes. In utero exposure to DDT has been linked to neurotoxicity and low birth weight, and miscarriages have been suggested by epidemiological studies. Studies have also suggested that DDT causes toxic effects to semen quality, menstruation, length of gestation, and may lower the duration of time that a mother is able to breastfeed. DDT is toxic to most animals and was made widely known through the 1962 book Silent Spring by Rachel Carson in which she exposed DDT for causing reproductive toxicity to a species of birds, which resulted in egg-shell thinning. This book is said to have facilitated the ban on DDT in the US in 1972.

DDT Regulation
Banned in United States. World Health Organization (WHO) and the US National Toxicology Program (NTP) classified DDT as moderately toxic and reasonably anticipated to be a carcinogen. The International Agency for research on Cancer (IARC) classifies DDT as possible human carcinogen. EPA classifies DDT, DDE and DDD as probable carcinogens.

Chlordane, Lindane and Toxaphene are chlorinated pesticides that were all used as contact pesticides (applied to animal skin, such as cattle dips). They are all now banned, but continue to be of concern due to their persistence in the environment. These pesticides bioaccumulate and they do not break down easily in the environment.

Chlordane
General Characteristics
Chlordane was introduced in 1948 and it was once used to treat agricultural crops such as corn. Chlordane is a synthetic organic chemical. It is a viscous liquid that varies in appearance from colorless to amber, with a faint chlorine-like aromatic odor. Chlordane is also known as chlordan and was manufactured in a white solid form. Chlordane is a chlorinated cyclodiene that was used widely before being banned in 1988. The only commercial application that is still approved for use in the US, according to the EPA, is for fire ant control in power transformers.

Chlordane Toxicity
Acute toxicity from chlordane exposure includes gastrointestinal and neurological toxicity. Chronic toxicity through inhalation of the pesticide is detrimental to the nervous system and it can be stored in fat cells. According to the EPA, one occupational exposure study has linked Chlordane to non-Hodgkin's lymphoma, while others have not linked it to this cancer. In humans, chlordane is a potent central nervous system toxicant. EPA has classified chlordane as a probable carcinogen.

Lindane
General Characteristics
Lindane (also known as benzene hexachloride, gamma-hexachlorocyclohexane, gammaxene and Gammallin) is another chlorinated cyclodiene pesticide that was banned by the EPA in 2006 for agricultural use. It is still approved by the FDA for use in the US in shampoos and lotions to treat lice and pubic (crab) lice and their eggs.

Children tend to get lice more often than adults and could be prescribed this type of topical treatment. Shampoos and lotions containing Lindane is generally prescribed when safer treatments do not work.

Environmental Exposure to Lindane

Lindane is a persistent toxin that is not easily removed from the environment. Lindane is a neurotoxin that can cause seizures as well as being toxic to the liver and kidneys. Lindane can weaken the immune system. Lindane is bioaccumulative. Lindane enters the atmosphere by becoming airborne during application as a pesticide, where it can travel long distances by wind transport. Lindane can leach from soil into surface waters and ground water and evaporates from water gaining access to the atmosphere contaminating rain or snow. Most personal exposures come from foods treated with lindane or homes in which lindane was used to control pests. These types of exposures have declined since its ban in the US in 2006. Lindane has been found in breast milk, but the concentrations have declined in direct correlation with the decline in agricultural application.

Toxaphene

General Characteristics

Toxaphene is another highly toxic, persistent and bioaccumulative chlorinated pesticide. It was used as a contact pesticide (applied directly to animal skin). Toxaphene was historically used in rivers and lakes to remove the "unwanted" fish for the sporting industry. Toxaphene contaminants evaporate into the atmosphere from contaminated surface waters and are carried long distances by the wind ending up in our rain and snow.

Toxaphene is a neurotoxin affecting the CNS through acute exposure. Several accidental deaths have occurred through acute ingestion of this toxicant. Toxaphene is toxic to the liver, kidney, adrenal gland and spleen and can accumulate in fat cells if people are exposed to chronic levels of toxaphene. Chronic exposure has also been shown to be a developmental toxicant (causing damage to unborn children), neurotoxicant, respiratory toxicant, and a possible carcinogen. Toxaphene was banned in 1986, but it was still used until 1990. Toxaphene-like pesticides are still made in parts of South Asia and Africa.

Environmental Exposure to Toxaphene
According to the EPA, we can still be exposed to toxaphene by consumption of contaminated shellfish, pineapples from Puerto Rico, bananas from the Virgin Islands, and eating other foods exposed to toxaphene. Babies can be exposed through breast milk and in-utero unborn babies can be exposed via the mother's bloodstream if she has been exposed to toxaphene. Toxaphene is still used as a cattle dip to control scabes.

Endrin
General Characteristics
Endrin is another pesticide whose use was banned in the United States. It has not been sold or produced since 1986. However, since it is a persistent environmental contaminant and will bioaccumulate, you may still be exposed to Endrin.

Endrin Toxicity
Endrin is primarily a neurotoxicant and most toxicity that has been noted is from acute exposures. Toxic effects from endrin are severe central nervous system toxicity to the brain and spinal cord and death. Accidental or intentional ingestion of endrin can lead to convulsions or death within minutes or hours of the exposure. Other visible symptoms of toxicity include confusion, nervousness, nausea, headaches and vomiting. Chronic toxicity has not been studied or noted in workers handling endrin.

Environmental Exposure to Endrin

You may be exposed to endrin in contaminated foods. If you live near a hazardous waste site endrin can contaminate your air, water and soil. Breastfeeding can expose infants to the toxicant, since endrin accumulates in fatty tissues. Endrin does not dissolve very well in water. It has been found in groundwater and surface water at very low levels. Endrin is more likely to adhere or stick to the bottom sediments of rivers, lakes, and other bodies of water. Endrin can enter the atmosphere by becoming airborne when it is applied agriculturally. A small amount of endrin does breakdown by exposure to high temperature or light which leads to the formation of the by-products endrin ketone and endrin aldehyde. Again this is a small portion of endrin in the environment and according to ATSDR endrin can remain in soil for more than ten years.

Endrin Regulation

Endrin has not been classified as a carcinogen according to the EPA. The regulatory limits for endrin in drinking water that are set by the EPA, are a maximum contaminant level (MCL) of 0.0002 milligrams per liter (mg/L). OSHA has limited the amount of endrin in air to 0.1 mg/m^3 for an 8-hour day per 40-hour workweek.

Deildrin and Aldrin

General Characteristics

Both of these toxic insecticides were used agriculturally throughout the world. Aldrin and deildrin are similar in chemical structure and they are often discussed together since aldrin breaks down to the chemical deildrin. Aldrin naturally breaks down to deildrin in living systems. In the environment, sunlight and bacteria break down aldrin into deildrin. Both of these pesticides are bioaccumulative. Unlike aldrin, deildrin is highly resistant to environmental breakdown. Aldrin was used as a pesticide on corn and potato crops for termite control. Deildrin was widely used as an insecticide on soil, fruits and seeds.

Environmental Exposure to Deildrin and Aldrin

Aldrin and deildrin may evaporate from soils contaminating the air and then be carried by wind to places far from the original point of contamination. Deildrin has a half-life of approximately five years in the environment. Exposure to these chemicals is primarily through the consumption of contaminated foods, such as seafood, fish, dairy, meat and root crops. Deildrin is present all over the environment at low levels. Aldrin rapidly changes to deildrin in plants and animals. Aldrin and deildrin were also applied to the basements of some homes for termite control. When purchasing an older home with a basement, an inquiry should be made as to whether or not these pesticides were applied.

Deildrin and Aldrin Toxicity: Aldrin and deildrin build up in the body, after years of chronic exposure. These chemicals are toxic to the nervous system. Animal exposure to deildrin has demonstrated nervous system toxicity as well as liver and immune system toxicity (a decrease in the ability to fight off infections). Deildrin and aldrin are not considered human carcinogens by the IARC, but they have caused cancer in mice liver. The EPA has classified both insecticides as probable human carcinogens. Aldrin is still used to control termites in Malaysia, Thailand, Venezuela and parts of Africa.

Chapter Summary

In this chapter we looked at some of the most important toxins and toxicants that we are routinely exposed to in our global environment. Some of these toxic chemicals have whole books dedicated solely to discussing that one particular chemical. The glimpse provided here into some of the thousands of toxins and toxicants, further demonstrates how complex toxicology is. There are many toxic chemicals that have yet to be identified or properly researched and characterized for their toxicity. However, having some insight into the chemicals covered in this chapter arm you with quite a bit of information about the toxic chemicals that you and your family may be exposed to.

6 Specialized Organs & Systems that help our bodies deal with Toxic Exposures

Our body has many specialized organs that allow our bodies to function while dealing with toxic exposures. Some of these major organs include the liver, the digestive gastrointestinal (GI) tract, the intestines, and the kidneys. The lung is our defense for airborne toxic compounds and particulates, while the lymphatic system is also a pathway for detoxification. The skin is our largest organ and is another barrier from toxins and toxicants. Many of us are aware of these vital parts of our body, but most of us may not fully understand how they function. Here we will learn how critical these organs and systems are for the protection of our body from toxic assaults.

I. The Digestive System

The digestive system consists of a set of organs that processes food from the time that it enters our mouth until it leaves our body. The digestive system includes the mouth, the esophagus, the stomach, the small intestine, the large intestine—also called the colon, the rectum, and the anus. The "gut" refers to the long digestive tract that starts at the mouth and ends at the anus. This twisting tube has many muscles that work to move food and produce enzymes and digestive juices that break down the food into "fuel" for our bodies many functions. In the hollow digestive organs – the mouth, the stomach, and the small intestine, is a specialized lining referred to as the mucosa which contains many tiny glands that produce juices to help digest food. The gut is also covered by a layer of smooth muscle that aid in food movement. There is also a gut brain, this neurological center functions very similarly to the brain and communicates directly with the brain. The digestive system is divided into major sections, the upper and lower portions.

The Upper Portion of the Digestive System (Mouth, Salivary Glands, Pharynx, Esophagus)

The Mouth & Salivary Glands – Where digestion begins!!

Digestion starts in the **mouth** and is aided by our sense of smell which triggers the action of the **salivary glands** in the mouth (your mouth waters). These salivary enzymes increase as you begin tasting your food. As you chew, your teeth physically tear the food into smaller pieces and, the salivary enzymes and digestive juices begin the food breakdown process so that it can be absorbed and transformed further as it travels down the digestive system.

The Pharynx and Esophagus – Food is on the move!

The **pharynx** is most commonly called the throat. The pharynx receives food from your mouth and swallowing occurs here. Swallowing is partially *voluntary* (under your control), when you choose to swallow your food and partially *involuntary* (controlled by the brain without your effort). The involuntary effort begins once you swallow. As the food prepares for swallowing it is formed into a ball-like mass called a bolus. The tongue and the soft palate of the roof of the mouth assist in pushing the bolus (ball of food) into the pharynx for swallowing. The epiglottis is the valve-like flap of cartilage behind the tongue that folds back to cover (and protect) the larynx to prevent food and drinks from entering into the windpipe (larynx). The pharynx branches into two organs the esophagus and the trachea (part of the respiratory system). The esophagus is the pathway for food travelling from the pharynx to the stomach. The trachea or windpipe carries air to the lungs (and is not a part of digestion).

The **esophagus** is a muscular tube that extends from the pharynx. The muscles of the esophagus contract and push the food down to the stomach. The esophagus is also known as the food pipe or swallowing tube. The muscle contractions that move food along are referred to as peristalsis. At the end of the esophagus is a muscular ring which is the lower esophageal sphincter (LES). The LES muscle will open to allow food to pass into the stomach and close to keep the stomach acid out of the esophagus. When the LES does not work properly, acid will enter into the esophagus and burn the esophageal lining which is a condition known as acid reflux or Gastroesophageal Reflux Disease (GERD). GERD is the leaking of food or acidic liquid backwards from the stomach to the esophagus.

The Lower Portion of the Digestive System (Stomach, Small Intestine, Colon, Rectum, Anus)

The Stomach and Small Intestine

The **stomach** (belly or tummy) is an organ that is shaped like a sack. The stomach contains a very strong acid (gastric acid) that continues to break food down. The stomach stores food and mixes it with gastric acid to change it into a liquid or paste form. Gastric acid has a pH of 1.5–3 and is composed primarily of potassium chloride (KCl) and sodium chloride (NaCl) and a small amount (about 0.05%) hydrochloric acid (HCl). Gastric acid is important in protein digestion through the activation of digestive enzymes and it causes proteins to unravel so that long chain amino acids can also be broken down. The portions of food that cannot be liquefied are passed on to the intestines for elimination from the body. The stomach also has a ring-shaped sphincter muscle called the pyloric sphincter. The pyloric sphincter or valve allows food to be passed from the stomach into the small intestine.

The **small intestine** is comprised of 3 segments – the duodenum, jejunum and the ileum. The small intestine uses enzymes released by the pancreas and bile released from the liver to further break down food. Peristalsis, the rhythmic movements that we mentioned earlier in the digestive tract, works here as well to push food along and mix it with the pancreatic enzymes and bile. The **duodenum**, the 1st segment of the small intestine is responsible for the majority of food breakdown that occurs in the small intestine. The 2nd segment – the **jejunum** and 3rd segment – the **ileum** are responsible for absorption of nutrients from food and delivery of these nutrients into the bloodstream.

There are finger-like projections in the small intestine that are referred to as villi, which give the small intestine a large surface area to absorb nutrients from food. It is here where the first pass effect, or elimination of some toxic chemicals can take place. When toxins and toxicants are not absorbed in the small intestine, they are not available to enter the bloodstream and cannot have a toxic effect on the body, unless they are directly toxic to the intestines. The first pass effect is how many toxins or toxicants are effectively removed from our bodies as leftover waste that moves on to the large intestine (lower GI tract).

The Colon, Rectum, and Anus

The colon (large intestine) is a long muscular tubule that measures 5-7 feet in length. The 4 portions of the colon are (1) the right or "ascending colon" (here is where the appendix is attached), (2) the middle or "transverse colon" and (3) the left or "descending colon", finally (4) the "sigmoid colon" (s-shaped) connects to the rectum. The colon processes waste so that excretion or defecation can occur. Peristalsis again comes into the picture by moving the waste (stool) through the colon. The stool is a mixture of bacteria and food debris. As stool moves through the colon, excess water is absorbed. The bacterium in the stool helps to process food particles and extract nutrients from vitamins and minerals. The sigmoid colon, stores the stool, until a movement empties it into the rectum (generally 1-2 times per day). The process of stool movement through the colon will usually take 36 hours.

The rectum is a hollow chamber that is approximately 8 inches long, once it receives stool from the colon, it stores it there and sends a signal to the individual's brain letting them know that it is time for elimination of the stool. Once the conscious decision is made to expel, the anus (sphincters) contracts to expel the stool. The anus consists of 2 sphincters (internal and external) and pelvic muscles, which create an angle between the anus and the rectum in order to stop stool from exiting when it should not be. The internal sphincter remains tight until stool enters the rectum, the external sphincter holds in contents until we decide to release.

The Gut-Brain (Enteric Nervous System) – Our Brain for Digestion

The enteric nervous system or gut-brain is quite similar to the larger brain that is located in the head. Many people do not realize that the gut-brain even exists. The gut-brain sends and receives neurological signals and impulses with the same nerve cells and neurotransmitters that are used by the brain. The gut-brain also responds to emotions and records experiences. The gut-brain is located in the tissue that lines the esophagus, stomach, small intestine and colon. The enteric nervous system is comprised of a network of neurons, neurotransmitters and neuropeptide proteins that communicate messages between the neurons.

Many gastrointestinal disorders are traced to issues with the gut-brain (such as irritable bowel syndrome – IBS). The gut contains over one hundred million neurons. The major neurotransmitters (serotonin [regulates appetite, sleep, well-being, happiness], dopamine [regulates movement and emotion], glutamate, norepinephrine [a hormone and neurotransmitter involved in stress response as well as mood regulation], nitric oxide [NO – possible regulation of water and electrolytes]) are found in the gut-brain, similar to the brain. Although seratonin is produced in the brain, 90% of the body's seratonin is found in the digestive system.

Depression and other diseases are attributed to deficiencies in seratonin levels. With the majority of drugs designed to target seratonin levels, neuro-gastroenterologists are looking at their effect on seratonin levels in the digestive tract. Conversely, toxicity that affects the digestive system may lead to deficiencies or disorders in neurotransmitters that can affect mood. Neuropeptides (proteins found in the brain) and immune system cells, endorphins (naturally occurring chemicals that reduce pain and affect mood to cause euphoria or a natural high) and benzodiazepines (an anxiety relieving chemical – like valium) are all found in the gut-brain.

The enteric nervous system functions independently of the central nervous system for the most part, but does communicate with the central nervous system routinely. The gut-brain is an independent type of circuitry that allows for digestion to take place without instructions from the brain. The vagus nerve is the connector between the brain and gut-brain. The brain sends signals to the gut-brain's interneurons (message carriers). Command neurons in the gut-brain control the activity of the gut and the vagus nerve controls the rates of neuron firing. There are sensors that monitor the progress of digestion and a form of a blood-brain barrier that protects the gut-brain's neurons from toxic agents. Over stimulation of the gut-brain can cause diarrhea. The gut-brain can also shut down or slow the colon leading to constipation. Communication between the brain and gut-brain is two-way; meaning that the gut brain can send signals up to the brain (like pain or gas bloating), as well as the brain sending signals down to the gut.

The gut brain will react to psychological drugs or any toxic agents that affect the nervous system. Psychological drugs can cause digestive malfunctions since they act on seratonin, recall that seratonin is also in the gut brain so therefore these drugs can cause digestive problems such as constipation or diarrhea. People suffering from neuro-degenerative diseases like Alzheimer's, also have digestive problems since the nerve cells in their gut-brain are affected by the disease, just as the nerve cells in the brain are.

There is research being conducted on how the gut-brain reacts to psychological drugs as well as determining what the psychological and "learning-capacity" of the gut-brain is. Experts in neurogastroenterology and neuroenteric scientists are studying these aspects and more including how the gut-brain mirrors emotions of the brain and how a person's emotions are affected by the state of the gut-brain. As more is discovered, more can be applied to the toxicological effects on the enteric nervous system.

II. Specialized Detoxification Organs

In this section we will cover the major detoxification organs. These organs play roles in multiple systems but they deserve special emphasis due to their roles in toxicity. We will also cover some of the diseases that can affect these organs.

The Liver

The liver is the organ that is designed to keep metabolism at a steady state in the body. The steady state is referred to as homeostasis. The main job of the liver is to filter blood from the digestive tract before it travels to the rest of the body. The liver makes proteins that are vital for a number of bodily functions such as blood clotting. The liver is a major chemical detoxifier and drug metabolizer. The liver secretes bile as it performs these crucial functions. Bile secreted by the liver ends up in the intestines. The liver is situated on the right side of the abdomen and is very close to the intestinal tract and pancreas. The liver is physically protected by the rib cage. On average the human liver weighs approximately 3 lbs (1.4 kg) and is divided into 2 sections, the right and left lobe. You can already start to imagine that if the liver starts to malfunction and disease ensues, the consequences to the body can be catastrophic.

Diseases of the Liver

Some of the known major diseases of the liver are:

Ascites: Ascites is a fluid that the liver leaks into the belly as a result of cirrhosis (liver cell death leading to liver damage). As ascites enters the stomach it will becomes distended and heavy.

Cirrhosis: Long-term damage to the liver from any cause that can lead to permanent scarring is called cirrhosis. The liver then becomes unable to function

Gallstones: If a gallstone becomes stuck in the bile duct draining the liver, hepatitis and bile duct infection (cholangitis) can result

Hepatitis: Hepatitis is the inflammation of the liver and it is generally caused by a set of viruses (Hepatitis A, B or C viruses). Some other causes for development of hepatitis include lifestyle factors such as excessive alcohol consumption, drug abuse, gallstones, allergic reactions, or obesity.

Hemochromatosis: Hemochromatosis allows iron to deposit in the liver thereby damaging it. The iron will subsequently deposit throughout the body, causing many other health problems.

Liver cancer: The most common type of liver cancer, hepatocellular carcinoma, almost always occurs after cirrhosis is present.

Liver failure: Liver failure has many causes including infection, genetic diseases, and excessive alcohol consumption.

Primary biliary cirrhosis: In this rare disorder, an unclear process slowly destroys the bile ducts in the liver. Permanent liver scarring (cirrhosis) eventually develops.

Primary sclerosing cholangitis: A rare disease with unknown causes, primary sclerosing cholangitis causes inflammation and scarring in the bile ducts in the liver.

Diagnostic Tests to detect Toxicity, Damage, Disease or Malfunction of the Liver

The following are some of the diagnostic tests that examine various biomarkers (biological indicators) for liver damage, disease and/or malfunction:

ALT (Alanine Aminotransferase): Elevated levels of ALT is an indicator of liver damage and helps diagnose liver disease or damage

AST (Aspartate Aminotransferase): Elevated levels of AST are an indicator of liver damage. ALT and AST are usually tested at the same time.

Alkaline phosphatase: Alkaline phosphatase is present liver cells that secrete bile; High levels of alkaline phosphatase indicate that the flow of bile out of the liver is not functioning properly and indicate that the liver may be blocked.

Albumin: The protein albumin is screened to aid in determining how well the liver is functioning.

Ammonia: Elevated ammonia levels in the blood are a direct sign that the liver is malfunctioning.

Bilirubin: Elevated levels of bilirubin indicate that the liver is not functioning properly.

CT scan (computed tomography): A CT scan of the abdomen gives detailed pictures of the liver and other abdominal organs for diagnosis of damage or disease.

Hepatitis A tests: Used to diagnose Hepatitis A (HepA) by screening for the presence of antibodies for the HepA virus as well as liver function.

Hepatitis B tests: Hepatitis B (HepB) is diagnosed by testing for the presence of antibodies for the HepB virus along with liver function.

Hepatitis C tests: Hepatitis C (HepC) can be diagnosed by testing for the presence of antibodies for the HepC virus along with testing the liver function.

Liver biopsy: A biopsy is a physical sample of the liver which is usually obtained and tested after another test (biomarker or imaging) indicates a possible liver problem

Liver function panel: A liver function panel checks how well the liver is working and consists of many different blood tests.

Liver and spleen scan: This nuclear scan uses radioactive material to help diagnose a number of conditions, including abscesses, tumors, and other liver function problems.

Ultrasound: An abdominal ultrasound can test for many liver conditions, including cancer, cirrhosis, or problems from gallstones.

The Kidneys

The kidneys are a set of 2 organs that are situated in the back of the abdomen. Each kidney is approximately the size of a fist or 4–5 inches (10 – 13 cms) in length. The kidneys filter blood from the body. All of the blood in our body will be filtered through the kidneys many times per day. Nephrons are the highly-efficient microscopic filters in the kidneys (the kidneys contains about one million nephrons) that filter urine. It is possible to lose as much as 90% of nephron function and still not lose the ability to effectively filter blood.

The filtration of blood through the kidneys allows for the removal of wastes (including toxins and toxicants), regulation of electrolytes and control over the balance of fluid in the body. The waste collected from the blood that is filtered by the kidneys ends up in urine which travels to the pelvis section of the kidney. Urine is used to test for the presence of toxicants and can be an indicator of damage or disease in the body. The urine drains from the kidney's pelvis to the ureters (tube like structures) and on the bladder.

Diseases of the Kidney

The following are some of the known diseases of the kidneys. People can live without one kidney; however toxicity to the kidney that causes its failure is catastrophic.

Acute renal failure: A fast and sudden loss of kidney function. This type of kidney failure can be brought on by a blockage in the urinary tract, dehydration or some type of physical damage to the kidney. This condition can generally be reversed.

Chronic renal failure: A permanent, partial-loss of kidney function which is commonly a result of high blood pressure or diabetes.

Diabetic nephropathy: Damage to the kidneys which is caused by high blood sugar from diabetes. It can lead to chronic kidney disease and nephrotic syndrome (this is a condition in which protein is found in the urine).

<u>End stage renal disease (ESRD)</u>: Total loss of kidney function, generally caused by progressive chronic kidney disease.

<u>Glomerulonephritis</u>: Kidney damage and inflammation caused by immune system malfunction (usually overactive) attacking the kidney and leading to kidney failure which is indicated by blood in the urine.

<u>Hypertensive nephropathy</u>: Kidney damage which results from blood pressure. This can lead to kidney failure.

<u>Interstitial nephritis</u>: Inflammation of the kidney's connective tissue which can lead to acute renal failure. This can be caused by chemical toxicity (drugs) or allergic reactions.

<u>Kidney cancer</u>: Renal cell carcinoma is the most common cancer of the kidney. Smoking is the most common cause of kidney cancer.

<u>Kidney stones (also called nephrolithiasis)</u>: Crystals (stones) formed from minerals found in the urine. The stones can be so large that they block the flow of urine. Some can be passed naturally by the body, while larger stones require medical treatment and/or surgical removal.

<u>Minimal change disease</u>: This is a form of nephrotic syndrome in which kidney cells look almost normal under microscopic examination; hence there is "minimal change" in their appearance. The disease can cause significant edema (swelling) of the leg.

<u>Nephrogenic diabetes insipidus</u>: The loss of the kidney's ability to concentrate the urine. Symptoms include thirst and frequent urination and may be brought on by drug toxicity.

Nephrotic syndrome: Kidney damage that leads to large amounts of protein being released into the urine. Edema (swelling) of the leg is a symptom of this disease.

Papillary necrosis: Severe kidney damage can lead to sections of kidney tissue breaking off internally and can clog the kidneys resulting in kidney failure.

Polycystic kidney disease: A genetic condition resulting in large cysts in both kidneys that impair their function.

Pyelonephritis: a bacterial infection of the kidney pelvis which is commonly caused by an untreated bladder infection.

Renal cyst: A hollow space in the kidney that is benign (non-threatening) which rarely impairs the function of the kidney.

Diagnostic Tests to detect Toxicity, Damage, Disease or Malfunction of the Kidney

The following are some of the diagnostic tests that examine various biomarkers (biological indicators) for kidney damage, disease and/or malfunction:

Computed tomography (CT scan): A CT scan is a series of X-ray images that are combined by a computer to create detailed images of the kidneys.

Kidney biopsy: A biopsy of the kidney is taken using a needle inserted into the back. A small piece of kidney tissue (biopsy) is removed. The kidney tissue is then examined under a microscope for diagnosis of a kidney problem.

<u>Kidney ultrasound</u>: ultrasound uses a probe placed on the skin which reflects sound waves off of the kidneys, creating images on a screen. Ultrasound can reveal blockages in urine flow, stones, cysts, or suspicious masses in the kidneys.

<u>Magnetic resonance imaging (MRI scan)</u>: A scanner uses radio waves in a magnetic field to make high-resolution images of the kidneys.

<u>Urinalysis</u>: A routine test of the urine, in which microscopic analysis of the urine is conducted in order to help detect infections, inflammation, microscopic bleeding, and kidney damage.

<u>Urine and blood cultures</u>: Cultures are grown from blood and urine. This will help diagnose a bacterial infection that is present and the type of bacteria causing the infection.

<u>Ureteroscopy</u>: An endoscope (flexible tube with a camera on one end) is put through the urethra and into the bladder and ureters. Ureteroscopy can help diagnose and treat conditions that also affect the ureters, but does not generally reach the kidneys.

The Pancreas

The pancreas is a gland located in the abdomen between the spine and stomach and is also partially located near the small intestine. The pancreas is very important to the digestive and the endocrine (hormonal) systems. As an endocrine organ the pancreas produces many important hormones including glucagon and insulin. As a digestive organ the pancreas secretes digestive enzymes (that aid in the further breakdown of fats, proteins and carbohydrates) and pancreatic juices that assist in the absorption of nutrients from food in the small intestines.

The pancreas has two types of cells. For digestion – the **acini cells** connect to ducts for secretion of pancreatic juices and enzymes into the small intestine. For the endocrine system – the **Islets of Langerhans cells** secrete the hormones of the endocrine system and are divided into 4 types of cells (α, β, δ and PP). The alpha (α) cells secrete glucagon, which increases blood glucose, the beta (β) cells secrete insulin, which decreases blood glucose, the delta (δ) cells control the stop and start of the α and β cells. The PP cells secrete pancreatic polypeptides (regulates the secretion activities of the pancreas for digestion and endocrine functions; PP contains 36 amino acids).

Diseases of the Pancreas

There are many diseases of the pancreas. Since it houses digestive enzymes and produces blood sugar regulating hormones, toxicity damage or disease to the pancreas is very serious. Here we cover some of the diseases of the pancreas.

Cystic Fibrosis (CF): CF also known as mucoviscidosis is a hereditary disease of the mucus and sweat glands which primarily affects the lungs, pancreas, liver, intestines, sinuses and sex organs, but can affect the entire body. CF changes the consistency of mucus to sticky and thickened. The disease is progressively disabling and eventually leads to death. Symptoms vary and can begin at birth or later in children and teenage years. CF can lead to pancreatitis.

Diabetes Mellitus (Type 1 & Type 2): Diabetes mellitus are a group of diseases of the pancreas in which there is a defect in insulin production, insulin secretion or both, which results in high blood sugar.

- ⅄ Type 1 Diabetes Mellitus (juvenile diabetes, insulin-dependent diabetes). During type 1 diabetes, your pancreas does not make insulin (decreases blood sugar). Without insulin, an abnormal amount of sugar (glucose) remains in your blood. As this condition remains, high blood glucose can lead to toxicity to the heart, eyes, kidneys, nerves, and gums and teeth. Symptoms include extreme thirst, frequent urination, weight loss, extreme hunger, chronic fatigue, blurry vision, sores that heal very slowly, dry and itchy skin, tingling feet or loss of feeling in feet.

⋏ Type 2 Diabetes Mellitus (Adult onset diabetes, non-insulin dependent diabetes): This disease is a result of a combination of resistance to insulin action and inadequate insulin secretion. Type 2 diabetes patients are not absolutely dependent upon insulin to sustain life, like type 1 diabetics are. Type 2 diabetics still have some ability to secrete insulin from the pancreas, but may also be treated with insulin to make up for the deficiency. Type 2 diabetes is often brought about by poor diet and lifestyle choices. It was formerly referred to as adult onset diabetes, because it was not diagnosed until adulthood. Most type 2 diabetics are diagnosed after 40, but the disease has been diagnosed more often in kids due to their diet, inactivity and obesity. Type 2 has been diagnosed in patients as young as two years of age when there is a family history of diabetes. People who are pre-diabetic for type 2 diabetes, can generally correct their diet and lifestyle and avoid a full diagnosis. Symptoms of type 2 diabetes are similar to type 1 diabetics – extreme thirst, blurry vision, frequent urination, extreme hunger or extreme fatigue, slowly healing wounds.

⋏ Diabetic Ketoacidosis (DKA) is a complication that normally affects those with type 1 diabetes but can also affect type 2 diabetics. This condition occurs when the body responds to a shortage of insulin by burning fatty acids and produces acidic ketone bodies (ketone bodies are formed as a byproduct of fatty acid breakdown). Symptoms can include vomiting, dehydration, breathing problems, and potentially lead to coma. DKA is normally onset when type 1 has not previously been diagnosed or if the diabetic is non-compliant with insulin therapy. DKA can be fatal if not treated immediately.

Pancreatitis: Inflammation of the pancreas in which the pancreas' digestive enzymes digests the pancreas itself. There are two forms of pancreatitis – acute or chronic. Both forms are serious and can lead to complications. Acute pancreatitis comes about quickly and usually goes away after a few days. Generally, the acute form is caused by gallstones. Symptoms include severe pain in the upper abdomen, nausea, and vomiting. Chronic pancreatitis is much more serious since it does not heal. Over time the disease leads to permanent damage of the pancreas. The most common cause for the chronic form is caused by heavy alcohol use. High levels of calcium or fat in the blood can also cause this disease. Symptoms usually consist of nausea, vomiting, weight loss, and oily stools.

Pancreatic cancer: Each type of cell in the pancreas (digestive or endocrine) can develop into a tumor. The most common type of cell that forms a tumor is the cell that lines the ducts. There are Islet cell tumors which can be benign or malignant (cancerous). These tumors will produce excessive amounts of hormones that are released into the bloodstream.

Diagnostic Tests to detect Toxicity, Damage, Disease or Malfunction of the Pancreas

Amylase and lipase: These biomarkers can be measured through a blood test. Elevated levels of these pancreatic enzymes can suggest pancreatitis.

Chapter 6: Specialized Organs & Systems

Computed tomography scan: A CT scanner takes multiple X-rays, and a computer creates detailed images of the pancreas and abdomen. Contrast dye may be injected into your veins to improve the images.

Endoscopic retrograde cholangiopancreatography (ERCP): A flexible lighted tube (endoscope) is combined with an x-ray to create pictures. The endoscope is passed through the mouth to the intestine so that the head of pancreas can be accessible for diagnosis or treatment by very small surgical tools that are passed through the endoscope.

Genetic testing: Many different mutations of a single gene can cause a disease affecting the pancreas such as cystic fibrosis. Genetic testing can help identify if an adult is an unaffected gene carrier or if a child will develop cystic fibrosis.

Magnetic resonance imaging (MRI): Magnetic waves create highly detailed images of the abdomen. Magnetic resonance cholangiopancreatography (MRCP) is an MRI that focuses on the pancreas, liver, and bile system.

Pancreas biopsy: Either using a needle through the skin or a surgical procedure, a small piece of pancreas tissue is removed to test for cancer or other conditions.

Physical examination: A mass on the pancreas may be detected by physically pressing the center of the abdominal area.

Sweat chloride test: A sweat sample is taken to measure chloride levels (elevated levels are indicative of cystic fibrosis). The skin is stimulated to sweat by a painless electric current.

Ultrasound: ultrasound probe is placed on the belly, and sound waves reflect off of the pancreas and create imagery for diagnosis.

Gallbladder

The gallbladder is a small pear-shaped organ that is located under the liver. The gallbladder is a storage sac for excess bile. Bile is a fluid made by the liver to digest fat; bile that is made in the liver travels to the small intestine via the bile ducts. If the intestine does not need the bile, it will travel into the gallbladder. Here the bile will wait for a signal from the intestines that food is present. Bile serves two main purposes. First, it helps absorb fats in the diet and secondly, it carries waste from the liver that cannot go through the kidneys. The gallbladder is an organ that your body can live without and it is removed when people have gallbladder problems. The most common issue with the gallbladder is a gallstone, which blocks the flow of bile.

Diseases of the Gallbladder

The following are some of the known diseases of the gallbladder.

Biliary Dyskinesia: (Acalculous cholecystopathy) is a gallbladder disease without the presence of gallstones, which causes pain to the upper right quadrant. This condition may also be referred to as impaired gallbladder emptying or functional gallbladder disorder.

Cholangitis: is inflammation of the bile duct. Acute cholangitis is generally due to bacterial infection resulting in bile becoming stuck in the duct. Symptoms include pain, fever, chills, jaundice, dark urine, pale stool and abdominal cramps.

Cholecystitis: Inflammation of the gallbladder. Acute cholecystitis is nearly always due to gallstones but can be due to a bacterial infection or irritation caused by chemical toxicity. Chronic cholecystitis can occur with or without gallstones being present.

Choledocholithias are gallstones in the bile ducts. Gallstones cause pain and varying symptoms depending upon the location of the blockage.

When the gallstone is in the neck of the gallbladder it will cause inflammation and distention and is referred to as cholecystitis. If the gallstones are in the common bile duct then bile can accumulate or may backup in the liver which can cause pancreatitis or obstructive jaundice. Symptoms include pain, fever, jaundice, dark urine, pale stool and chills.

Cholestasis: is the loss of bile flow in the small bile ducts or large bile ducts. This disease can lead to bile entering into circulation which may cause skin irritation, itching, jaundice, dark urine, pale stool, fat in the stool and blood clotting impairment.

Gallbladder Cancer: cancerous tumors in the gallbladder are usually detected once the gallbladder is removed for another reason, such as gallstones. There are rarely symptoms associated with gallbladder cancer in its early stages and if diagnosed, it is generally advanced. Women are more susceptible than men to developing gallbladder cancer and Native Americans are much more likely to develop gallbladder cancer than white Americans.

Gallbladder Polyps: growths that stick out of the lining of the gallbladder. Most of the polyps are non-cancerous (about 95% are benign) and are rarely found to be malignant (cancerous). Most polyps develop due to cholesterol deposits. Generally there are no symptoms associated with gallbladder polyps and are detected during an ultrasound to diagnose some other medical issues. While gallbladder polyps are rarely painful, they can occasionally grow large enough to need surgical removal.

Diagnostic Tests to detect Toxicity, Damage, Disease or Malfunction of the Gallbladder

The following diagnostic tests can detect gallbladder toxicity:

Abdominal X-Ray can show visual evidence of gallbladder disease such as gallstones.

Complete Blood Count (CBC) test looks at levels of various blood cells to indicate infection or other anomalies of the gallbladder.

Computed tomography (CT) scan constructs X-ray images of the abdominal organs to show visual evidence of gallbladder damage, disease or toxicity.

Endoscopic retrograde cholangiopancreatography (ERCP) is conducted by placing a tube (endoscope) down the throat, through the stomach and into the small intestine. Dye is injected through the tube in order to show the gallbladder, liver, and pancreas on X-ray. Treatment can be conducted by passing tiny surgical tools through the endoscope.

Hydroxy iminodiacetic acid (HIDA) scan or cholescintigraphy: is an injection of a radioactive material which is taken up by the gallbladder in order to measure the organ's function.

Liver function tests (LFTs): is a blood test that can detect evidence of gallbladder disease.

Magnetic resonance cholangiopancreatography (MRCP): utilizes magnetic resonance imaging (MRI) which shows detailed imagery of the gallbladder.

Ultrasound: ultrasound testing uses sound waves that reflect the image the gallbladder for diagnosis.

Specialized Organs that deal with inhaled toxins and toxicants: The Respiratory System

Inhaled toxins and toxicants can be solid (particles), gaseous or liquid in forms. The respiratory organs are the body's specialized organs that deal with inhaled toxic agents. In this section we learn about the respiratory organs that help your body combat airborne toxins and toxicants.

The Upper Respiratory System

The upper respiratory system or upper airways include the nose (nasal passages and nasal cavities) and the pharynx. The function of the upper respiratory system is to filter, warm, and moisten air before it gains entry into the lower respiratory system.

The Nose

The nose has two nasal cavities and is the point of entry for most airborne toxins and toxicants (a portion can be ingested through the mouth). The nasal cavities (or nostrils) are lined with hair-like projections referred to as cilia. The cilia will trap larger particles as waste and even make some smaller particles larger by adhering them to other larger particles. Cilia will also trap some gaseous/liquid toxins and toxicants. When the nose traps toxins and toxicants here, they are generally no longer a threat to the body and are removed through swallowing or nasal waste.

The Pharynx (shared with the digestive system)

We talked about the pharynx (throat) as a part of the digestive system, now we will look at the pharynx in regards to respiration. The throat has 3 parts, the nasopharynx, oropharynx and laryngopharynx. Each part essentially describes the portion of the throat that is attached to another organ. Nasopharynx is just above the soft palate and is the airway from the nostrils. The nasopharynx contains the adenoids (tonsils) and the openings to the auditory (estaquian) tubes. The oropharynx is the portion of the throat extending from the soft palate to the epiglottis (base of the tongue) and the laryngopharynx is the narrow portion between the hyoid bone of the larynx and the entrance to the esophagus.

The Lower Respiratory System

The lower respiratory system includes the larynx, trachea, bronchi and lung. When toxins and toxicants are able to get into the lower airways and into the lung, they are more likely to cause toxicity to the lung or one of the lower respiratory organs.

The Larynx

The larynx or voice-box is the airway to the lungs. The larynx regulates the opening to the lower respiratory system and produces sound. It is a two inch long tube in the neck, made up of the hyoid bone and several cartilages (thyroid, cricoid and arytenoid). This is where the vocal cords reside. Each time we inhale or exhale, through the nose or mouth, toxins or toxicants move through the larynx, to the trachea and then to the lung.

The Trachea

The trachea extends from the base of the larynx and splits off to form the bronchi and connects to the right or left lung. The trachea is a tubular structure that is approximately 4 ¼ inches long by 1 inch wide. The trachea is located behind the esophagus.

The Bronchi

As the trachea splits into the right and left primary bronchi, which are called the extrapulmonary bronchi, they enter the lung at a groove called the hilus. Each primary bronchus branches into smaller and smaller passageways to move air deeper into the lung. The branches of the primary bronchi are called secondary bronchi or intrapulmonary bronchi. The smallest passageways are the bronchioles.

The Lung

The lung is a pair of two organs that is collectively referred to as the lungs. The lungs are located in the center of the chest, one on either side of the thorax separated by the heart and protected by the rib cage. The right lung has three lobes (superior, middle and inferior) and the left lung has two lobes (superior and inferior). The lungs are spongy, elastic, lightweight and porous. Visceral pleura (enclosed space that encases the lungs similar to a balloon) covers the surface of the lungs as well as surfactant cells that secrete an oily coating that prevent the alveoli of the lung from sticking together. Alveolar cells (or alveoli) have a wall that contains macrophages. The macrophage is very important in dealing with toxicity. These are the cells that engulf or "eat" debris, toxins and toxicants. This process is called phagocytosis, if macrophages are not able to phagocytize the foreign species, then it may be able to cause damage to the lung.

The lung receives air (oxygen containing) through inhalation and expires air (de-oxygenated) by exhalation. A person can breathe either through their mouth (oral) or nose (nasal), which is why people are referred to as oro-nasal breathers. When you are born the lung is pink in color. As you age it becomes gray, as your lung traps the dirt and debris that you have inhaled.

Diseases of the Lung

The following are a few diseases of the lungs that can be caused by toxins and toxicants.

Acute bronchitis: An infection of the airways that appears suddenly. It is generally caused by a virus.

Asthma: Persistent inflammation of the airways which leads to spasms that occur along with wheezing and shortness of breath. Toxins, pollutants, infections and allergies will trigger asthma.

Cancer: cancer can develop in any part of the lung but most commonly occurs in or near the air sacs in the main part of the lung.

Chronic bronchitis: a chronic cough which is a form of chronic obstructive pulmonary disease (COPD).

Chronic obstructive pulmonary disease (COPD): the inability to exhale normally, which results in the difficulty breathing.

Emphysema: damage to the lungs' connections between alveoli which causes air to be trapped in the lungs, thereby making exhaling difficult.

Mesothelioma: A rare form of lung cancer that develops on the lungs' pleura, which is generally caused by exposure to asbestos.

Pneumonia: An infection of the alveoli, usually by a bacterial toxin.

Pulmonary Edema: Fluid leaking from the lung's small blood vessels into air sacs and the surrounding space in the lung. Pulmonary edema can be caused by back pressure, heart failure and direct injury to the lung.

Tuberculosis: a form of pneumonia that is caused by the bacteria toxin *Mycobacterium tuberculosis*; this form of pneumonia progresses slowly.

Pneumoconiosis: refers to a category of lung conditions that are caused by inhalation of toxicants that cause lung injuries.

Size Distribution – Particulate Deposition in the Lung

The size of a particle or particulate matter will determine how deeply it will settle into the airways and lungs. Particulate matter refers to solid particles or liquids that are distributed in a gas. In the environment and workplace, particulate normally refers to dusts, particles, mists or fumes that are suspended in air. Particles can deposit in the lung by diffusion, impaction, interception and sedimentation. **Diffusion** is random motion of fine particles that are < 0.5 μm. These particles will deposit on lung walls, small airways and alveoli. The motion of these particles becomes more vigorous the smaller that they are in size. **Impaction** occurs when a bend in the airways takes place and the particle settles or impacts to a surface in the lung along its original airway path, not in the direction of the airway bend. Particles that are 10 μm or greater tend to be deposited by impaction in the nasopharynx, due to the high speed airflow and bends in air. **Interception** of a particle takes place when it travels close to the surface and touches that surface; most fibers (like asbestos) are deposited by interception. **Sedimentation** occurs when gravity and air-resistance overcome the particles tendency to float, which results in surface settling. Sedimentation occurs most often in the bronchi and bronchioles.

Size Distribution Table – Location that particles tend to settle in the lung is based upon size (method of deposition may vary).

Particle Size	Area of Deposition	Method of Deposition
>10 μm	Upper Airway Nasopharyngeal Region	Impaction
0.003 – 5 μm	Trachea, Bronchial, Bronchiolar, Alveolar Regions	Sedimentation

0.5 μm or less	Alveolar Region (Smaller branches of lung and the air exchange area)	Diffusion
<0.001 μm	Upper airways Nasopharyngeal Region	Impaction

Skin – The largest organ and physical barrier from toxins and toxicants

The skin is the largest organ of the human body. It makes up about 16% of our body weight. Not only does the skin envelope our bodies to support our posture and keep our internal temperature optimally set (homeostasis); one of its greatest features is the protection that it provides to multiple systems in our bodies. Skin is waterproof and is a barrier to toxins and toxicants. Recall early on that the least effective route of toxicity is the skin. This does not mean that certain toxins and toxicants cannot enter through the skin (percutaneous absorption). Skin toxicity is referred to as cutaneous toxicity. The toxic chemicals that can undergo cutaneous absorption and get into circulation must have certain characteristics which make them more likely to cross the dermal barriers (recall that solvents readily cross the skin barrier). There are three major layers of the skin that form the protective barrier (epidermis, dermis and hypodermis).

Layers of the Skin

The **epidermis** is the outermost layer of the skin and there are 5 layers of epidermis. The outermost layer is the stratum corneum (also called the horny layer) which is composed of dead skin cells. The thickness of the epidermis varies depending upon its location on the body; it is the thickest on the soles of the feet and palms of the hands. The stratum corneum layer of the epidermis sheds regularly about every 2 weeks, in fact we have a cloud of shedding skin cells that are around us constantly. This cloud cannot be seen under normal light. It is estimated that we lose approximately 1 million dead skin cells in a 24 hour period (they accumulate in the dust around our homes) and that we shed approximately 8 lbs (3.6 kg) of dead skin annually. The epidermis has specialized cells keratin cells which are called keratinocytes. Keratinocytes are generated at the bottom layer – the stratum basale of the epidermis which is located at the point where the epidermis attaches to the dermis (desmosomes attach the epidermis to the dermis). The keratinocytes make new column shaped skin cells that move to the surface of the epidermis at the stratum corneum layer, this process takes about 1 month (ranges 4–6 weeks). As these cells move up they become progressively flatter and once at the surface the skin cells die and are sloughed off. Also in the epidermis is the melanocyte, which forms melanin. Melanin imparts color to our skin and hair; this pigment is produced by the melanocytes and makes up approximately 5% of the epidermis. The epidermis also houses some of the Langerhan cells which are critical for immunity; these cells detect foreign cells such as toxins and toxicants, capture these toxics and deliver them to the lymph nodes in the dermis for immune response of the lymphocytes. Langerhan cells are made in the bone marrow and comprise roughly 2–5% of the epidermis. The other specialized cells of the epidermis are the tactile cells that are referred to as the Merkel cells. Merkel cells are involved in touch and are mechanoreceptors. Merkel cells make up roughly 6–10% of the epidermis and are located near the keratinocyte renewal layer and are attached to a nerve ending. Merkel cells can be isolated or grouped in bunches, these clusters of cells are called merkel corpuscles.

The **dermis** is comprised of 80% water, collagen, elastic tissue and reticular fibers that float in a glycoprotein gel. The dermis' main functions are support for the skin, temperature regulation, repair and defense. The dermis has two layers and varies in thickness depending upon its location in the body, yet it ranges from 10–40 times thicker than the epidermis. The upper layer of the dermis (papillary layer) is comprised of the major cells of the dermis – the **fibroblasts** which produce the protein fibers **collagen** (provides support and strain resistance) and **elastin** (gives skin elasticity). The collagen fibers are arranged in a thin layer in the dermal papillary and are perpendicular to the surface of the skin. Collagen makes up 70% of the proteins in the dermis. The lower layer of the dermis (reticular layer) is a thicker layer of collagen fibers that are arranged in multiple directions. The dermis has several specialized cells and structures. The hair follicles are located here and each follicle is attached to a muscle (erector pili). A network of nerves and blood vessels are networked throughout the dermis layer and transmit signals to the brain for detection of itching, temperature changes and pain. Glands are also located in the dermis. The scent (apocrine) and oil (sebaceous) are located in the hair follicles and the sweat (eccrine) glands are located elsewhere in the dermis. Other specialized nerve cells that transmit signals of pressure and touch are the Meissner's and Vater-Pacini corpuscles.

The **hypodermis** (subcutaneous) is the innermost layer of the skin. This folds into the dermis and is attached to it by collagen and elastin fibers. This layer is made up of fat storing cells (adipocytes/adipose) and connective tissue. This layer is important for regulating the temperature of the body and skin. The adipose cells can release stored fat (and any accumulated toxins and toxicants) back into circulation during times of starvation or fat-burning. The thickness of the hypodermis varies depending upon its location in the body and the sex of the individual. Women tend to have thicker hypodermis layers around the hips, thighs and buttocks (below the waist) and men tend to have thicker hypodermis layers above the waist over the abdomen and shoulders.

Chemicals can enter the skin at varying rates. Toxicants that weaken or destroy the surface layers of the skin can easily gain entry (acids, bases/caustics). Other chemicals weaken the stratum corneum and pass on to the dermis of the skin gaining access to veins and circulation. There is varying information regarding whether or not hair shafts allow entry of chemicals since skin with very little to no hair has roughly the same rate of absorption for chemicals. The hair follicle route would be highly inefficient and is considered insignificant. This route may only facilitate slow penetrating chemicals. The easiest route for chemical entry is through wounds, scrapes or cuts in the skin. These breaks in the protective layers ease access to the dermis. Household detergents and solvents can dry the skin, causing cracking and facilitate the entry of toxicants. Chemicals that cause hives, skin flaking or ulcerations weaken the stratum corneum and also make us vulnerable to toxicant entry. While some solvents can soften the stratum corneum, many cannot penetrate much farther down the epidermis, unless there is prolonged contact (extended duration) exposure. Some stronger chemicals such as benzene, methyl alcohol or carbon tetrachloride easily pass through the epidermis and gain entry into blood circulation. Aside from chemical structure and composition and integrity of the skin, the location of the exposure and water content of the epidermis and temperature at that site also influence how well a chemical will be absorbed by the body.

Diseases of the Skin

Some of the diseases of the skin are caused directly by exposure to toxins and toxicants. Here we review some common skin diseases including some occupational skin disorders (OSD).

Acne: acne is the most commonly seen skin disorder which can be caused by multiple reasons (stress, genetics, and hygiene). It can also be caused by exposure to toxins and toxicants in the air accumulating on the surface and penetrating into the sebaceous glands and causing surface inflammation and development of a pustule or deep inflammation which leads to a papule (pimple) or very deep inflammation that will cause a cyst to form. If oil from the surface gland breaks through to the surface the result are whiteheads and if the oil accumulates melanin pigment and is oxidized a blackhead will appear at the surface. Acne can also be caused by drugs including prescription drugs such as hormones – oral and injected, lithium, and iodides.

Cancer: Skin cancer is generally caused by exposure to ultraviolet radiation, but it can also be caused by exposure to other toxicants (polyaromatic hydrocarbons such as tar or coal). Smoking has been attributed as one cause of oral skin cancer.

Dermatitis/Eczema: Irritant contact dermatitis is also knows as eczema. This is inflammation of the skin which results from exposure to a toxicant. This is the most commonly reported OSD. There are 2 categories of contact dermatitis. Irritant contact dermatitis (ICD) is a non-immunological response and the inflammation is generally localized at the site of contact following exposure to a toxicant. ICD accounts for approximately 80% of all reported OSD contact dermatitis cases according to the CDC. Allergic contact dermatitis (ACD) is an immunological response resulting in inflammation of skin after exposure to a skin allergen. Generally, this is caused by previous exposure to a toxicant that has caused chemical sensitization (common skin sensitizers are pesticides, metals, resins and certain solvents). The reaction is not contained at the site of contact and may cause systemic responses and toxicity.

Fungal Diseases: skin fungal diseases can be caused by a variety of fungal toxins (example ringworm/tinea) and can occur in several places on the skin. These skin diseases tend to occur most often in dark moist places such as the feet. They are also commonly seen in nail beds, particularly under synthetic nails. Symptoms vary depending upon the type of fungus, but most commonly skin discoloration, itching and odor will occur.

III. Systems that circulate throughout the body: delivery and removal of toxins & toxicants (The Circulatory and Lymphatic Systems)

The Circulatory System (Blood and Blood Cells)

The circulatory or blood system is a network of blood vessels (arteries, capillaries and veins) that spans throughout the body. The system is highly organized and uses vessels and muscles to regulate the flow of blood through the body. The main parts of the circulatory system are the heart, arteries, capillaries and veins and lung. The circulatory system has 3 systems – the pulmonary (lung – movement of blood from the heart to lung and back to heart), coronary (heart – movement of blood through the tissues of the heart) and systemic (system – nourishment to all tissues throughout the body), which all must work on their own in order for the entire circulatory system to work. The circulatory system's main function is to transport nutrients, water, and oxygen (O_2) to the billions of cells in the body, while removing waste and carbon dioxide(CO_2) produced by the body's cells.

The blood is pumped by the heart, which forces the blood through the body. The blood leaves the left ventricle and travels into the aorta as oxygenated (red in color) blood. The blood travels through thousands of miles of blood vessels within your body. As the blood travels back to your heart it is rich in CO_2 and waste and is blue in color (it is deoxygenated). The blood contains bloods cells and plasma. The blood cells are the red blood cells (rbc), white blood cells (wbc) and platelets. There is approximately 5 liters of blood flowing throughout the adult human body.

The blood vessels consist of arteries, capillaries and veins. Arteries are the vessels that carry oxygenated (oxygen rich) blood away from the heart. Capillaries are the tiny blood vessels that are thinner than human hair. Capillaries connect arteries to veins. Nutrients from food, oxygen, and waste travel in and out of blood circulation through the walls of capillaries. Veins carry deoxygenated, carbon dioxide rich blood back towards the heart.

Red blood cells (rbcs) are responsible for oxygen and carbon dioxide transport. There are approximately 5 million rbcs in one drop of blood. RBCs become oxygenated in the lungs and transport the oxygen to all of the body's cells. After rbcs deliver O_2 to the cells it takes up the CO_2 and transports the CO_2 back to the lungs where it is removed from the body by exhaling.

White blood cells are critical for the attack on germs, infections and foreign invaders. When the body has an infection, the production of wbcs is increased. Typically, there are approximately 10,000 wbcs in one drop of blood. Platelets are blood cells that assist in stopping bleeding. There are approximately 250,000 platelets in one drop of blood. Platelets stick to damaged blood vessels at the opening in order to attract more platelets, fibers and other blood cells to seal the injury and stop bleeding. A scab is the platelet "plug". Plasma is made in the liver and is the liquid portion of the blood. Plasma carries the blood cells and other components through the body's expansive circulatory network.

Diseases of the circulatory system

The diseases of the circulatory system are diverse since they can affect the lung, heart and blood. Here we will focus on some of the major blood disorders.

Anemia: decrease in all 3 types of blood cells (white blood cells, red blood cells and platelets). Most commonly, anemia is a deficiency of the red blood cells. Anemia can also occur if there is a depletion of hemoglobin (Hb), which is an iron-rich protein that gives blood its red color and helps red blood cells to carry oxygen from the lungs to the rest of the body. During anemia you do not receive enough oxygen rich blood which leads to symptoms of fatigue. Long-term anemia can lead to organ damage of the brain, heart or other organs. Severe anemia can be fatal. Some types of anemia can be prevented with a healthy diet or dietary supplements.

Myeloma: Cancer of the plasma cells. In myeloma, the plasma cells overgrow, forming a mass or tumor that is located in the bone marrow. During myeloma, the abnormal plasma cells eventually invade and destroy the outer, hard layer of bone. The types of myeloma are classified by the type of immunoglobulin produced by the abnormal plasma cells. Myeloma is the second most common blood cancer, but it is not a commonly diagnosed cancer.

Sickle Cell Anemia: the most common form of sickle cell disease (SCD). SCD is a serious disorder in which the body makes sickle-shaped red blood cells. "Sickle-shaped" means that the red blood cells are shaped like a crescent. Sickle cells contain abnormal hemoglobin called sickle hemoglobin or hemoglobin S. Sickle hemoglobin causes the cells to develop a sickle, or crescent, shape. Sickle cells are rigid and sticky. Sickle cells tend to block blood flow in the blood vessels of the limbs and organs. Symptoms from blocked blood flow can cause pain, serious infections, and organ damage. Sickle cell disease is inherited and there is no cure. The gene must be inherited from both parents in order for sickle cell disease to develop.

The Lymphatic System (Soft Tissue)

The lymphatic system is also referred to as the soft tissue system. The lymph "bathes" the organs of the body. Lymph literally means clear water and it is the fluid and protein from the blood plasma. The lymphatic system is a network of lymphatic vessels throughout the body, similar to the blood system. However, unlike the blood system it is not a closed system; the vessels are not pressurized and are not controlled by a pump (heart). The network carries lymph fluid, nutrients and waste material between the blood stream and the tissues of the body. The movement of lymph occurs despite the low-pressure environment and this movement of lymph is influenced by everyday activity such as muscular and skeletal movement or the everyday motion or activity of the body. The less movement that a person undergoes, the lower the lymphatic movement will be. The lymph fluid is filtered by lymph nodes (small glands) that are located throughout the body. The lymph nodes are 1-2 cm (0.4 – 0.8 in) in size and are shaped like a bean. The lymphatic system produces lymphocytes which are immune cells that help defend the body against disease and toxicity. As the filtering of lymph fluid takes place, the lymph nodes will trap toxic substances, bacteria, virus and other foreign agents. After trapping them, it will destroy them with white blood cells – and is why the lymphatic system is so important for immunity. If a certain part of the body is infected, lymph nodes that are located in that region will collect the infection and swell. Many people have seen or experienced swollen lymph nodes in their neck when they have a throat infection. If the lymph or soft tissue is infected with a disease such as cancer, it can spread the cancer from one part of the body to other parts of the body.

Lymphatics are in every part of the body with the exception of the central nervous system. The lymphatic system also absorbs lipids (fat) from the intestine and delivers it to the blood. Most chemical toxicants are fat soluble, meaning that those chemicals that are absorbed by the fat that is in the small intestine can be delivered to the blood circulatory system by lymphatics.

Diseases of the Lymphatic System

Castleman Disease: There are 2 types of castleman disease – localized and multicentric. Localized castleman disease affects one region of lymph nodes in the stomach and chest. Symptoms include pain and pressure in the stomach and difficulty breathing. Multicentric castleman disease affects more than one region of lymph nodes and lymphoid-containing organs. Symptoms include sweating, weight loss, fever, night sweating fatigue and can lead to nerve damage which presents as symptoms of numbness and weakness.

Chapter 6: Specialized Organs & Systems

<u>Lymphatic filiaris</u>: is a disease in which parasitic worms infiltrate the lymph system through a mosquito bite. Symptoms are generally not seen, but swelling of the breasts, legs or genitals may occur when lymph fluid collects in one area due to a block of flow caused by parasitic worms obstructing the vessels. People diagnosed with lymphatic filiaris are prone to frequent infections. Other notable conditions that develop are thickening and hardening of the skin and in certain cases, lymphatic filiaris can lead to tropical pulmonary eosinophilia (TPE) syndrome, a condition characterized by wheezing, shortness of breath, coughing and nighttime wheezing.

<u>Lymphedema (Lymphatic Obstruction)</u>: this is swelling due to increased fluids or obstruction of the lymphatics. Lymphedema can be caused by cancer, an inherited abnormality of the lymphatics, infection, scar tissue that is formed from radiation treatments or the surgical removal of lymph nodes.

<u>Lymphoma (Hodgkin's Disease & Non-Hodgkin's Lymphoma)</u>: These forms of cancer are a group of cancers affecting the lymphocytes (white blood cells located in the lymphoid organs). They are classified as blood cancer. Lymphomas fall into one of two major categories: Hodgkin's lymphoma (HL, previously called Hodgkin's disease) and all other lymphomas (non-Hodgkin's lymphomas or NHL). HL and NHL can occur in the same places and may have the same symptoms and may also have similar appearance during a physical examination. They are distinguishable through microscopic examination. HL develops from a specific abnormal B lymphocyte lineage. NHL may develop from either abnormal B or T cells and are identified by unique genetic markers. There are 5 subtypes of HL and 30 subtypes of NHL. NHL occurs more commonly than HL in the US. Lymphoma is the most common blood cancer in the US and it is also the 7th most common cancer in adults and 3rd most common in children. The risk of developing NHL increases with age.

<u>Mesenteric lymphadenitis</u>: is inflammation of the lymph nodes that result from an intestinal infection. Symptoms include right lower stomach pain, fever, nausea, vomiting, diarrhea and fatigue. This disease is often mistaken for appendicitis due to the similarity in symptoms and it will typically affects children and adolescents.

Chapter Summary

In this chapter we gained knowledge about our highly specialized organs and systems that our bodies are equipped with to deal with toxic insults from multiple routes of exposure. Since toxicity can occur anywhere in our body, it is important to understand not only how these organ and systems work to combat toxic insults, but also how toxicity to any of these organs or systems will lead to disease or damage. We are fortunate that there are many ways to assist in diagnosing toxicity, damage or disease, but it is critical to pay attention to the signals from your body, so that you are able to seek diagnosis and treatment. It is important to note that several of the diseases or toxic responses discussed in this chapter can be prevented or corrected by lifestyle changes, in particular modifying nutrition (diet), reducing stress and incorporating exercise.

7 Food Toxicology: The Complexity of Sustenance

We view our food as so much more than just sustenance. Food is pleasurable, psychological, cultural, emotional and spiritual. From a scientific perspective, particularly from a toxicological view, food is highly complex chemically. Food Toxicology is the study of the nature, properties, effects, and detection of toxic substances in food, and their disease manifestation in humans. The scientific complexity of food is due in part to the very nature of food. In its natural state, agriculturally grown food contains essential vitamins and minerals that our bodies need while also containing an array of chemicals that can vary in amounts based upon how and where the food was grown. Food, unaltered, is not homogeneous (or consistent) in taste quality and texture. However, the demand for consistent flavors, colors and texture has led to alterations in nature's formula for food. This can stem from a farmer selecting particular seeds from selected fruits or vegetables or breeding certain animals that have preferred physical and taste characteristics to the use of genetically modified (or genetically engineered) organisms and foods. How these unnatural alterations affect our bodies long-term is still in question and up for much debate; clues are beginning to emerge from anecdotal reports and epidemiological studies. These areas of concern cross into the specialty of nutritional toxicology (this specialty will be discussed in our next chapter).

The Regulation of Food

In the United States and in several other countries, food is regulated by a central agency that is given that authority and responsibility. The US has the Federal Food, Drug and Cosmetic (FD&C) Act, which gives the federal government authorization to ensure that all food and foodstuffs involved in interstate sales is safe. The Act is sufficiently broad since the extent to which safety can be proven is not absolute; therefore this law allows for food to be presumed safe. In other words a vegetable or animal meat is presumed safe unless a toxic or harmful substance in an amount that has been shown to cause adverse health effects is detected.

If this Act was too detailed and attempted to regulate the hundreds of thousands of naturally occurring substances and compounds in food (and more that form once cooked), this would not only be cost prohibitive, it would be too time consuming. Fresh produce and meats would age under delays imposed by regulations, would not arrive to the consumer as quickly and as such could very easily result in food shortages. Therefore, it is wise to presume that the freshly harvested foods that you can purchase from your farmer's market or grocery stores are safe.

Much of what we know about foods came long before regulations, regulatory agencies (Food and Drug Administration – FDA or the U.S. Department of Agriculture – USDA) or the chemical content of foods was known. Common sense and experience with foods that are safe to eat must be considered so that we can continue to enjoy the foods that we love. The FD&C Act allows for reasonable approaches to the assessment of food, food ingredients, additives, and contaminants for safety. Food additives that are not inherently found in food are regulated quite differently from naturally occurring substances. Food additive chemicals and substances receive much more scrutiny. Food can be rendered harmful if any of these substances make food toxic to health and must meet higher safety standards.

Safety, as defined by the USDA and FDA, for substances added to foods, allows for farmers and food companies to easily understand how much of an additive (color, flavor, nutrient and food) they can safely add to the foods that they process. The safety of the chemicals focuses on the nature of the substance and the intended conditions of use or, as stated in the FD&C Act, "safe for intended conditions of use". The safety of these chemicals is based upon dosage (quantity) of the ingredient and their expected use and presence in the diet.

It is important to note that natural foods and additives contain a great number of trace impurities and even amounts that are undetectable by testing. Therefore chemical limits in food are set for toxic contaminants in order to protect the health of consumers. Again, these limits must be simple to understand so that food companies and processors can confidently ensure that they are not exceeding safety limits. As some of you may be aware, these regulations while meant to protect all may not cover every person. People with inherent food allergies and food allergies that develop later in life, learn by trial and error (unless they have had an allergy screen) that certain foods should not be a part of their diet. There are many examples of people who eliminate certain classes of foods altogether, and note improvements to their overall well-being. One example is the elimination of gluten containing foods for those suffering from Celiac disease (gluten causes an immune attack on the nutrient absorbing villi of the small intestines).

The Complex Nature of Food

The very nature of food imparts its unique chemical composition. The majority of these chemical compositions have yet to be characterized or isolated. This is especially difficult since food is heterogeneous (not uniform) or varies in its natural state. Food is necessary for living and functioning and many of us regard food very highly and look at it as more than just fuel to keep us moving. Foods importance can be marked in all cultures and throughout history. Special events or occasions are celebrated with certain foods that have cultural and spiritual significance.

Food toxicology is so distinctive because food simply cannot meet the same rigorous standards for uniformity and purity as other manufactured items. While food is so much more heterogeneous (inconsistent) in chemical content than other items, it is the class of products to which we have the greatest exposure to. Foods are grown and harvested from so many different environments, soil and water, which have been contaminated with directly added chemicals (such as pesticides, herbicides, etc.) and indirectly added chemicals from rain, runoff and bioaccumulated sources. Food toxicology and food science assesses safety by analyzing normal and modified/added constituents of food and how our bodies will absorb, distribute, metabolize and excrete the ingested substances.

We mentioned that food contains minerals and vitamins that are essential to the way our body functions and ultimately our health and well-being. These vitamins and minerals can also be toxic at too high doses, so when adding these essential ingredients to our foods, those limits must be placed so that we receive the beneficial dose as opposed to the toxic dose. These components or micronutrients are part of the non-caloric value of foods; they add no caloric value to food, but they are still essential for living. The other nutrients in our food that make up the majority of food composition and have caloric value are carbohydrates, fats and protein (macronutrients).

Non-nutrients include naturally occurring substances, food additives, contaminants and products of food processing/manufacture. While most people may believe that non-nutrients come from food processing, nature provides the majority of non-nutrient constituents. The US Code of Federal Regulations (CFR), Chapter 21, section 170.3(o), has 32 categories of direct food additives. Of these 32 categories, there are approximately 3000 substances: 1800 are flavor additives which are already naturally occurring and non-nutritive and about half which are added at levels that are found naturally (21 CFR 170.3(o); Cassaret and Douls). Many non-nutrients may be essential for the growth of the plant, including natural pesticides and hormones while others may be toxic or anti-nutrients (such as goiterogens, i.e. thyroid suppressing foods, enzyme inhibitors or mineral binding substances that slow or decrease the body's absorption of these minerals).

Generally Recognized as Safe (GRAS)

The FD&C Act has allowed additives into our food if these substances perform a distinct function (nutritive or non-nutritive) and are determined to be generally regarded as safe (GRAS) by scientists trained in food safety. The additives on the GRAS list are presumed safe and are not regulated. The non-regulation is due to either the long-term experience with the substances (common use in foods) or evidence produced by scientific procedures for adequacy of safety. The FDA and other non-agency scientific experts can make GRAS determinations for additives, but they all must consistently make the determination based upon specified scientific procedures and experience based upon common use prior to January 1, 1958 as stated in the FD&C Act. Non GRAS ingredients can also be added but these additives are regulated. These non GRAS ingredients must be approved by the FDA prior to any addition to food that is sold, marketed or distributed to the public.

Food that contains unavoidable contaminants is not automatically deemed unsafe. However, if a food does contain unavoidable contaminants, even with the use of current good manufacturing practices (CGMP) that are proven to be harmful to health then they are deemed unfit for consumption. CGMP are followed by pharmaceutical and biotechnology industries in order to ensure that the products produced meet specific requirements for identity, strength, quality, and purity.

Provisions of the law for additives that contain unavoidable substances can be regulated for the protection of public health, by limiting the allowed quantity (referred to as a tolerance). In other words a limit on the amount of unavoidable contamination is set as a tolerance or an informal action level, which does not have the strength or enforcement of the law.

Contaminants that are found to be avoidable and have adverse health effects that are considered toxic are referred to as "unfit for human consumption" or "adulterated". If consumers are already in possession of foods containing these contaminants, alerts must be made that are based upon the health risk posed by the contaminated foods. Those causing serious adverse health effects or fatality, receive the greatest warning, highest recall and most follow up (US - Class I recall) as prescribed by 21 CFR 73.

Color additives are dyes, pigments or other substances that are made either by a synthesis process or extracted and isolated from a vegetable, animal or mineral source. A color additive's only function is to impart a color to a food. Other food additives can have multiple functions. Food color additives are classified by two distinct categories. Exempt food colors are those that are derived from natural sources and thus are non-regulated. There are approximately 25 exempt food colors and they generally are not tested as extensively as their regulated/synthetic counterparts. The second category is comprised of the synthetic food colors that require certification. These are the majority of regulated food color additives which are approved for use and have the prefix "FD&C" – for example, FD&C Yellow #5. Orange B and Citrus Red No.2 are the only certified food colors that do not have the FD&C prefix (21 CFR 74 Subpart A). These color additives contain structures that cannot be synthesized without a number of impurities and subsequently must be carefully tested, monitored and certified as safe prior to use in food products (Casarett & Doull's). Color additives are not eligible for the GRAS list. Regulated food colors are considered non-toxic and more widely used than natural exempt colors. This is in part due to natural colors lacking chemical and color stability. Natural colors will fade with time, and often, more of these natural food colors are needed to achieve consistent coloring. Hence, most of our processed foods are colored with synthetic food coloring. Beverages account for the highest use of synthetic foods colorings, followed by candies and confections.

Dietary Supplements

Supplements are viewed as foods and food-type substances, not as food additives or drugs. Therefore, while a food ingredient must demonstrate safety, a supplement must demonstrate "no history of unsafe use" (this standard of proof is much easier to meet). Supplements cannot make unapproved health claims and if they do, they would then be regarded as a drug and would be subject to the same regulation, demonstration of safety, and efficacy of a drug.

Food Allergies

Food allergies (hypersensitivity) are immune reactions to consumed food. Hypersensitivity reactions can include dermal or cutaneous reactions such as a rash, hives (uticaria), dermatitis, eczema or a gastrointestinal response such as nausea, vomiting, diarrhea and abdominal cramps. Hypersensitivity can also include respiratory reactions such as wheezing, asthma, bronchospasm (sudden constriction of bronchiole walls) or rhinitis (runny nose, nasal inflammation or irritation, itching, sneezing, stuffy nose due to congestion or blockage). Other toxic hypersensitivity reactions to food include anaphylactic shock, hypotension, methemoglobinemia (a blood disorder in which an abnormal amount of methemoglobin is produced) and swelling of the tongue and larynx. Analphylactoid hypersensitivity reactions are seen as mimicking the action of anaphylaxis by histamine. Bronchospasms have been induced by sulfites in wine. Proteins in food are all subject to causing hypersensitivity, and there are several common food allergens that are documented.

Here is a list of some common foods that contain proteins that cause hypersensitivity reactions:

- Banana
- Codfish
- Cottonseed
- Egg Whites
- Egg Yolks
- Green Peas
- Guava
- Mandarin
- Milk (Cow)
- Okra
- Peach
- Peanuts
- Rice
- Shrimp
- Soybeans
- Tomato
- Wheat

Metabolic food allergies are separate from other food allergies, since these are commonly consumed foods that only show toxicity when improperly processed or ingested in excess amounts. Some diseases caused by metabolic food reactions include:

Amyotrophic Lateral Schlerosis (ALS) – disease of the nerve cells in the brain and spinal cord that control voluntary movement: caused by improperly processed or excessive consumption of cycads (cycads flour)

<u>Cyanosis</u> – blue or purple tinting of the skin: caused by improperly processed or excessive consumption of **lima beans, cassava roots, millet/sorghum sprouts, apricot and peach pits, bitter almonds**

<u>Goiter</u> – enlarged thyroid: caused by consumption of **cabbage family, soybeans, radishes, rapeseed, mustard seed, turnips**

<u>Hypertension, cardiac enlargement, sodium retention</u>: caused by improperly processed or excessive consumption of **Licorice (glycyrrhizic acid)**

<u>Intracranial pressure, irritability, death</u>: caused by improperly processed or excessive consumption of **polar bear, chicken liver**

There are wide arrays of foods that cause allergies. Food allergies can have severe toxic effects and even fatal consequences, therefore it is important to know whether or not you have food allergies.

Tolerance Levels for Food Substances

Laws and regulations require that toxic chemicals (pesticides, drugs used on animals used for food, and unavoidable contaminants) are set at concentration levels that will not cause harm to the consuming public. For pesticide residues, a safety factor is included that protects children and infants. For drugs used in animals the tolerance levels are based upon a toxic risk assessment that considers the metabolism and potency of the drugs on the animals and the human consumer. Some unavoidable contaminants are those that are ubiquitous in the air and that are food-borne contaminants. Most toxins in seafood are set at zero tolerance in the US, this is because most of these toxins are neurotoxins and result in severe or permanent toxic effects including fatality.

Chapter 7: Food Toxicology

<u>The following is a list of a few examples of Seafood or Marine Toxins</u>:

<u>Chelonitoxin</u>: sea turtle toxin; symptoms include cell death (necrosis) of the cardiac muscle (myocardium) and build-up of fluid in the air sacs of the lungs (pulmonary edema)

<u>Ciguatera toxin</u>: from dinoflagellates (*Gambierdiscus toxicus & Prorocentrum* species); associated with algal blooms. Ciguatera is bioconcentrated up the food chain into fish (contaminated tropical reef fish such as barracuda, grouper, sea bass, and mullet) that are consumed by humans. Symptoms include gastrointestinal toxicity – nausea, vomiting, diarrhea, cramps, profuse sweating, neurological toxicity, muscle aches, headache and death.

<u>Domoic Acid or Amnesic Shellfish Poisoning (ASP)</u>: found in mussels; associated with algal blooms; from a dinoflagellate (*Nitzschia pungens*). Symptoms include permanent or short-term memory loss; headache, disorientation, memory loss, inability to communicate, gastrointestinal distress, seizures, paralysis or death.

<u>Tetrodotoxin (TTX)</u>: in pufferfish (Fugu) is a delicacy in Japan; this potent neurotoxin causes paralysis of the central and peripheral nervous system, hypotension and severe gastrointestinal distress. TTX blocks the flow of sodium ions into nerve and muscle cells which is necessary for the conduction of nerve signals and impulses. 1-2 mg causes death and every year poisoning occurs when people who are not certified by the Japanese government to prepare pufferfish (remove the toxin) serve the dish to consumers. TTX is approximately 10,000 times more deadly than cyanide.

<u>Saxitoxin or Paralytic Seafood Poisoning (PSP)</u>: one of the most potent non-protein toxins known to man; 0.2 mg is fatal; saxitoxin is associated with algal blooms. Saxitoxin is found in shellfish and is also bioconcentrated from two species of dinoflagellates (*Protogonyaulax and*

Pyrodinium species). This potent neurotoxin blocks the flow of sodium ions into nerve & muscle cells; sodium ion flow is necessary for the conduction of nerve signals and impulses. Symptoms include tingling, burning sensation or numbness of face, lips and extremities (hands, feet); headache, floating sensation, temporary blindness, respiratory difficulty and death.

Mycotoxins are toxins made by various species of molds. Control of mycotoxin contamination in food is of utmost importance since they are the sources of the majority of foodborne illnesses in the world's developed countries.

Some examples of Mycotoxins produced by various molds in Foods:

Aflatoxins (B_1, B_2, G_1, G_2) – these toxins are made by the molds *Aspergillus flavus, Aspergillus parasiticus*: They are carcinogenic (cancer causing), and can cause acute poisoning (aflatoxicosis). This toxin is **found in corn, peanuts and other stored grains**.

Aflatoxin (M_1) – a metabolite of Aflatoxin B_1 (AFB1) – Hepatotoxin (liver toxicity). **Found in Milk.**

Citreoviridin – this toxin is made by molds *Penicillium citreoviride* and *Penicillium toxicarium*. Citreoviridin causes cardiac thiamin/Vitamin B1 deficiency (beriberi). **Found in Rice.**

Cyclopiazonic Acid – this toxin is made either by species of *Aspergillus* or *Penicillium*. Causes muscle, liver and splenic toxicity. **Found in cheese, grains and peanuts.**

Fumonisins B_1, B_2, B_3, B_4, A_1, A_2 – these toxins are made by the mold *Fusarium moniliforme*. Causes cancer (carcinogen). **Found in corn.**

3-Nitropropionoic acid – this toxin is made by the molds *Arthrinuim sacchari, Arthrinuim saccharic*ola and *Arthrinuim phaeospermum*. Causes central nervous system toxicity (impairment). **Found in sugarcane**.

Ochratoxin – this toxin is produced by the molds *Aspergillus ochraceus* and *Penicillium viridicatum*. Ochratoxin causes cancer (carcinogen) and chronic inflammation of the kidneys tubules and interstitium (Balkan nephropathy). **Found in grains, peanuts, green coffee**.

Patulin – this toxin comes from the mold *Penicillium patulatum*. Causes cancer (carcinogen) and hepatotoxicity (liver). **Found in apple and apple products**.

Chapter Summary

The complex nature of the biological and chemical makeup of food, directly contributes to the complexity of food toxicology. Food is a mixture of hundreds of thousands of biological and chemical substances, macronutrients and micronutrients (vitamins, minerals). Food is our fuel for survival and has a deep-rooted cultural and spiritual standing in many societies. Food is essential for all human survival and while it may seem counterintuitive to have regulations on our food, there are too many opportunities for food to become toxic or contaminated if not properly or consistently managed. It is also important to have an awareness of the naturally occurring toxins and the effect of man-made toxicants on our food supplies.

8 Nutritional Toxicology: Surviving in a Sea of Toxicity

History of Nutritional Toxicology

Nutritional toxicology is a sub-specialty of Toxicology and differs from food toxicology. Food toxicology deals with the amount of toxins and toxicants found in food that can cause harm or damage to humans. Nutritional toxicology focuses on how nutrients in food can counteract the toxic effects of toxins and toxicants.

The history of nutritional toxicology can be traced to early man as they learned to eat foods that would not harm them and found healing properties in some foods. Many medicines that were developed over time came from using foods and natural materials as medicine. Nutritional and food toxicology combine food science, toxicology and nutrition. Nutritional toxicology is an emerging science and its definition will continue to evolve as its scope expands.

There are very few nutrients that are found in natural food sources that will cause significant toxicity, with the exception of Vitamin A, Vitamin D and some other minerals. Potential sources of toxicity from nutrients generally come from dietary supplements. If these supplements are taken in too high doses, toxic effects can occur.

Deficiency Leads to Disease

Nutritional research has focused for years on understanding the effects of vitamins and minerals (micronutrients) found in foods and needed by our bodies for survival. Since deficiency of the required micronutrients will lead to toxic effects or disease, it is significant to food scientists to learn how these micronutrients play a part in the thousands of processes in our body. We have seen over the course of this book that there are many biological systems that allow our bodies to function properly and deal with toxins and toxicants. A micronutrient deficiency can and will lead to a loss of partial or total function of one or more bodily processes, organs or systems. Eventually, when our body can no longer make up for the deficiency, disease will develop. Here are some diseases that develop from deficiencies. So next time that you think that having the appropriate levels of vitamins and minerals in our diet is *not important*, think again!

Micronutrient Name	Diseases caused by deficiency
Vitamin A – Retinol	Night blindness, perifollicular hyperkeratosis, xerophthalmia, keratomalacia, increased morbidity and mortality in young children
Vitamin B1 – Thiamine	Beriberi (peripheral neuropathy, heart failure), Wernicke-Korsakoff syndrome
Vitamin B2 – Riboflavin	Cheilosis, angular stomatitis, corneal vascularization

Vitamin B3 – Niacin (Nicotinic Acid, Niacinamide, Nicatinamide, Vitamin PP)	Pellagra (dermatitis, glossitis, GI and CNS dysfunction)
Vitamin B6 (Pyridoxine, Pyridoxal, Pyridoxamine)	Seizures, anemia, neuropathies, seborrheic dermatitis
Vitamin B9 – Folate (Folic Acid, Folacin)	Megaloblastic anemia, neural tube birth defects, mental confusion
Vitamin B12 – Cobalamins	Megaloblastic anemia, neurologic toxicity (confusion, paresthesias, ataxia)
Vitamin C – Ascorbic Acid	Scurvy (hemorrhages, loose teeth, gingivitis, bone defects)
Chromium	Impaired glucose tolerance
Copper	Anemia, Menkes' syndrome (Sparse and coarse/kinky/steely hair, hair growth failure and degeneration of nervous system)
Vitamin D – Cholecalciferol, Ergocalciferol	Rickets, Osteomalacia (bone softening)
Vitamin E – alpha-Tocopherol (most active form in humans) and others beta-, gamma-, & delta-tocopherol; and alpha-, beta-, gamma-, & delta-Tocotrienol	Red Blood Cell (rbc) hemolysis (abnormal breakdown of cells), neurological toxicity
Fluorine	Tooth decay, Osteoperosis
Iodine	Goiter, Cretinism/Neonatal hypothyroidism (severe stunted mental and physical growth),

Iodine (cont.)	Deaf/Mutism, impaired fetal brain development and growth
Iron	Anemia, Pica(eating disorder – consuming a variety of non-nutritive substances such as clay or dirt), Glossitis (tongue inflammation), Angular cheilosis/cheilitis (lesion at corner of mouth)
Vitamin K – Phylloquinone, Menaquinones	Bleeding due to deficiency of prothrombin and other factors, Osteopenia (bone mineral density loss)
Manganese	Inhibition of collagen production, Skeletal deformation
Molybdenum	Tachycardia (pulse or heart rhythm disorder), Nausea, Obtundation (reduced level of alertness or consciousness)
Selenium	Keshan disease (viral cardiomyopathy/ heart muscle disease), Muscular weakness
Zinc	Impaired growth, Delayed sexual maturation, Hypogonadism (sex glands produce little or no sex hormones), Hypogeusia (reduced ability to taste)

Chapter 8: Nutritional Toxicology

Food as Medicine

"Let thy food be thy medicine and thy medicine be thy food", is a phrase that was coined by *Hippocrates* (460-377 B.C.), the ancient Greek physician who is considered the father of Western Medicine. Over the centuries, modern medicine has adopted medications derived from natural food sources (mostly plant based). Eastern and Western medicine vary widely in their use and application of natural-based therapies or medications. Eastern medicine widely employs what is viewed as alternative medicine and alternative therapies by Western medicine. So while the "father" of Western medicine coined the phrase, let thy food be thy medicine, there is much less emphasis on using diet and food for its medicinal purposes. That tide is beginning to change as more people, in Western Medicine practicing societies, are starting to turn to alternative therapies and treatments and using diet as preventative medicines. Medical professionals, scientists and regulatory agencies are responding to the demands of the public and toxicologists have been expected to come up with a reliable way to assess nutritional toxicity.

Globally, research on the use and extraction of compounds for the development of new drugs is not new. However, scientists are starting to take a closer look at (and conduct research on) the effects of genetic modification of foods on human health, the effect of diet on protection from toxicity (nutritional toxicology) and the effect of food on gene expression and genetic variation on how food is absorbed, distributed, metabolized and eliminated (nutrigenomics).

There is much that is now known in regards to the vitamin and mineral content of food and plant sources. Advances in food analysis gives people reliable information of the expected vitamin and mineral concentrations found in a variety of foods. However, when toxins and toxicants alter the nutritional value of agriculturally grown foods, it is not as easy to predict the variations in how beneficial these foods will actually be in regards to providing your body with the amount of micronutrients that are needed.

This decline in the quality of food has further complicated the issue. So while concentrations of the micronutrients found in foods may change, the following are a list of micronutrients (vitamins and essential trace minerals) and their sources in a variety of foods.

Micronutrient Name	Food Source
Boron (B)	beans, beer, cider, dates, green leafy greens, grains, prunes, dates, raisins, honey, nuts, some fresh fruit, wine
Calcium (Ca)	almonds, Brazil nuts, broccoli, buchu leaves, cabbage, carob, caviar, cheese, collards, dairy foods, dandelion leaves, dulse, figs, filberts, green leafy vegetables, kale, kelp, milk, molasses, mustard greens, oats, parsley, pau d'arco bark, prunes, salmon, sardines, seafood, sesame seeds, shrimp, soybeans, tofu, turnip greens, valerian root, white oak bark, yogurt
Chloride (Cl)	table salt, sea salt, kelp, olives, tomatoes, celery
Choline (B complex)	eggs, liver, milk, peanuts
Chromium (Cr)	apple peel, banana, beef, beer, blackstrap molasses, brewer's yeast, brown sugar, butter, calves' liver, cheese, chicken, corn, dairy products, dried beans, eggs, fish, liver, meat, mushrooms, oatstraw, oysters, potatoes with skin, seafood, shell fish, Stevia leaves, whole grains.
Cobalt (Co)	Beet greens, buckwheat, cabbage, clams, dulse, figs, goldenseal, Irish moss, kelp, kidney, lettuce, liver, milk, oysters, pau d'Arco, sarsaparilla, spinach, watercress
Copper (Cu)	alfalfa, almonds, avocados, baker's yeast, barley, beans, beet roots, black pepper, blackstrap molasses, Brazil nuts, broccoli, cashews, cocoa, crab, dandelion leaves, garlic, grapes, green leafy vegetables, green

Chapter 8: Nutritional Toxicology

Copper (Cu) cont.	olives, haddock, hazelnuts, herring, honey, horsetail, lentils, liver, lobster, molasses, mushrooms, mussels, nuts, oats, oranges, oysters, peanuts, pecans, radishes, raisins, sage, salmon, skullcap, seafood, sesame seeds, shrimp, soybeans, sunflower seeds, walnuts, wheat bran, wheat germ, white oak bark, yucca
Folic Acid (Folate)	dark, leafy vegetables; enriched and whole grain breads; fortified cereals
Fluorine (F)	apples, calves' liver, cheese, cod, eggs, kidneys, meat, salmon, sardines, seafood, seaweed, sodium fluoride, tea
Iodine (I)	asparagus, chard, cod, cod-liver oil, dulse, garlic, haddock, herring, iodized salts, Irish moss, kelp, lima beans, lobster, mushrooms, oysters, salmon, sea salt, seafood, seaweed, sesame seeds, shrimp, soybeans, spinach, squash, sunflower seeds, turnip greens
Iron (Fe)	almonds, avocados, beans, beef, beets, blue cohosh, bran, brewer's yeast, broccoli, butchers broom, cashews, caviar, cheddar cheese, chickweed, cocoa, dates, devil's claw, dried fruit, dulse (seaweed), eggs, egg yolk, garbanzo beans, green leafy vegetables, grits, spinach, heart, kelp, kidneys, legumes, lentils, liver, millet, molasses, mullein, mussels, oysters, parsley, peaches, pears, pennyroyal, pistachios, potatoes, poultry, prunes, pumpkins, raisins, rice, seaweed, sesame seeds, soybeans, sunflower seeds, tofu, tongue, walnuts, wheat bran, wheat germ, whole grains
Lithium (Li)	sugarcane, seaweed, natural mineral waters, tobacco
Magnesium (Mg)	almonds, barley, blackstrap molasses, bluefish, brewer's yeast, buckwheat, carp, cocoa, cod, cottonseed, figs, flounder, garlic, green leafy vegetables, halibut, herring, Irish moss, kelp, licorice,

Magnesium (Mg) cont.	lima beans, meat, mackerel, millet, molasses, nettle, nuts, oat straw, oats, peaches, peanut butter, peanuts, peas, perch, seafood, sesame seeds, shrimp, snails, soybeans, sunflower seeds, swordfish, tofu, wheat, wheat bran, wheat germ, whole grains
Manganese (Mn)	avocados, barley, beans, bilberry fruit, blackberries, blackstrap molasses, blueberries, bran, brown rice, buckwheat, buchu leaves, chestnuts, cloves, coffee, egg yolks, ginger, grapevine, green leafy vegetables, hazelnuts, kelp, legumes, nuts, oatmeal, peanuts, peas, pecans, pineapples, red raspberry leaves, rice bran, rice polish, seaweed, seeds, spinach, walnuts, wheat bran, wheat germ, whole grain cereals
Molybdenum (Mo)	barley, beans, buckwheat, cereal grains, green leafy vegetables, legumes, lentils, lima beans, liver, meats, milk, organ meats, peas, sunflower seeds, whole grains, yeast
Phosphorous (P)	Beef, bran, cabbage herb, cheese, corn, cocoa, cottonseed, dairy products, dog grass, eggs, fish, fruit, garlic, legumes, liver, meat, nuts, peanuts, poultry, pumpkin seeds, rice polish, squash seeds, soda, soybeans, sunflower seeds, wheat bran, wheat germ, whole grains
Potassium (K)	almonds, apricots, avocados, bananas, beef, bran, Brazil nuts, brewer's yeast, broccoli, brown rice, cabbage herb, cashews, celery herb, chard, citrus fruit, dairy foods, dates, figs, fish, fruit, garlic, grapefruit juice, green leafy vegetables, guava, legumes, lentils, meat, milk, molasses, nectarine, nuts, oranges, parsley, parsnips, peanuts, peaches, pork, potatoes, poultry, raisins, rice bran, sardines, seaweed, seeds, soybeans, spinach (fresh), squash, sunflower seeds, tomato juice, veal, walnuts, wheat bran, whole grains, yams.

Selenium (Se)	barley, beer, blackstrap molasses, bran, Brazil nuts, brewer's yeast, broccoli, brown rice, buchu leaves, butter, cabbage, catnip, celery, cereals, chicken, cider vinegar, cinnamon, clams, crab, cucumbers, dairy products, dog grass, eggs, garlic, grains, green leafy vegetables, hibiscus, ho shou wu root, kidneys, lamb, liver, lobster, meats, milk, milk thistle seeds, molasses, mushrooms, nutmeg, nuts, oats, onions, seafood, Swiss chard, tuna, turnips, wheat bran, wheat germ, whole grains
Silicon (Si)	alfalfa, beets, bell peppers, brown rice, dulse, Echinacea root, eyebright herb, goldenseal root, green leafy vegetables, horsetail grass, liver, soybeans, whole grains
Sodium (Na)	anchovies, bacon, beef, bologna, bran, butter, Canadian bacon, clams, corned beef, dulse, green beans, green olives, ham, Irish moss, kelp, margarine, meat, milk, poultry, rose hips, salt, sardines, seafood, tomatoes
Strontium (Sr)	trace amounts in foods (plant and animal based)
Sulfur (S)	beans, brussel sprouts, cabbage, clams, dairy products, eggs, fish, garlic, meat, milk, onions, soybeans, taurine, turnips, wheat
Vitamin A (Retinol)	carrots, fortified cereals, sweet potato with peel, spinach mango, broccoli, butternut squash, tomato juice, pumpkin, beef liver
Vitamin B1 (Thiamin)	Bread, whole grain, enriched, fortified products and cereals, spinach, green peas, tomato juice, watermelon, sunflower seeds, lean ham, lean pork chops, soy milk
Vitamin B2 (Riboflavin)	bread products, fortified cereals, milk spinach, broccoli, mushrooms, eggs, milk, liver, oysters, clams
Vitamin B3 (Niacin)	fish, milk, poultry, enriched and whole grain breads, fortified cereal spinach, potatoes, tomato juice, lean

Vitamin B3 (cont.)	ground beef, chicken breast, tuna, liver, shrimp
Vitamin B5 (Pantothenic Acid)	beef, chicken, cereals, potatoes, oats, tomatoes
Vitamin B6 (Pyridoxine)	fortified cereals, fortified soy products, organ meats, bananas, watermelon, tomato juice, broccoli, spinach, acorn squash, potatoes, white rice, chicken breast
Vitamin B7 (Biotin)	fruit, liver, meat
Vitamin B12 (Cobalamin)	fish, fortified cereals, meat, poultry, shellfish, milk, eggs
Vitamin C (Ascorbic Acid)	broccoli, citrus fruits, kiwis, mango, red and green peppers, strawberries, snow peas
Vitamin D (Calciferol)	fish liver oils, fatty fish, fortified milk products, fortified cereals
Vitamin E (alpha-tocopherol)	almonds, avocado, cod, fortified cereals, peanut butter, shrimp, sunflower seeds, sweet potatoes, tofu, vegetable oils, wheat germ
Vitamin K	broccoli, brussel sprouts; cabbage, collards, liver, spinach,
Zinc (Zn)	beans, beef, bilberry fruit, black strap molasses, brewer's yeast, buchu leaves, capsicum fruit, chicken heart, crab, egg yolk, fish, herring, lamb, legumes, liver, maple syrup, meats, milk, oysters, peanuts, pork, poultry, pumpkin seeds, ricotta cheese, skullcap herb, seafood, sesame seeds, soybeans, sirloin steak (lean), sunflower seeds, swiss cheese, turkey- dark meat, tofu, wheat bran, wheat germ, whole grains, yeast

Organic Foods: Free from toxins and toxicants?

Due to the ubiquitous nature of toxins and toxicants in our environment, even organic foods may be subjected to their toxic effects. Provisions are taken by certified organic farms to mimic a natural ecosystem. US organic farms can be transitioned from traditional farms to certified as organic after 3 years (immediately preceding harvest) of not applying prohibited materials (USDA National Organic Program - NOP). Recall that some toxic materials can persist for years and decades in the soil. Some farms who claim organic status are exempt from certification (small farms or those with less than $5000 in gross organic sales annually); farms can be converted field by field (with buffer zones for runoff, separate facilities and record keeping to prevent commingling of organic and non-organic foods). There are also some synthetic pesticides that are considered non-toxic and some synthetic fungicides that are approved for use on organically grown crops (on "The National List" part of the NOP Rule (sections 7 CFR 205.600 – 205.606).

In regards to certified organic animals for food, in the US the NOP states that animals can be converted to organic after 12 months of being under organic management. Animals can be converted at the same time that the land is converted to organic. Organic slaughter animals can come from any breeding stock that has been organically managed from the last third of gestation. A one-time exemption of all organic feed for conversion of an entire, distinct herd may be granted to permit feeding of up to 20% of non-organic feed for the first 9 months, followed by 100% organic feed for three months. If this type of conversion is made, all replacement animals must be managed organically from the last third of gestation. Poultry must be organically managed from the second day of life. There is one approved parasiticide, Ivermectin, which is on "The National List"

While organic foods are not all created equally, they are generally the safest option available to the average consumer. The USDA is the certifying body for the NOP. However, concerns have been raised by consumers and scientists regarding testing frequency and abuse by dishonest groups. There have been several cases of organic foods and products that have been tested and found to contain toxic chemicals. It is important to remain educated and vigilant when choosing foods and other products, be them organic or non-organic.

Food as a source of Toxicity

While our bodies do a great job of combating much of these toxic mixtures, there comes a point when our system starts to give out and health issues begin to manifest in the form of symptoms. How many times have you (or someone that you know) taken a pain pill for an unknown ache or pain, and never bothered to have that symptom properly evaluated? Many people self-medicate to alleviate symptoms, even when these symptoms return on a recurring basis. While over the counter medications may be an option for treating minor symptoms, it is always best to consult your medical professional. Generally, people who turn to diet or are prescribed changes in diet, are already headed towards toxic effects, are already showing signs of toxicity or are close to development of a life-threatening disease. It is well documented that cholesterol levels, and type 2 diabetes mellitus can be prevented by changes in diet and exercise. A highly nutritious diet can counteract damage that has been brought on by years of a poor diet. While certain people are using foods to heal, many others, in the medical industry and in the general public, still do not view food choices as critical to health and longevity. There are many factors that may influence the course taken (diet and/or medication) with each individual patient and caregiver. Toxic exposures can be very difficult to diagnose and in many cases undetectable for years. This is why when you choose either to self-medicate or to supplement your diet with vitamins and minerals, it is crucial for you and your health care professionals to have open communication. If you have a good health-care professional s/he should be open to a comprehensive conversation that includes discussing symptoms, diet, supplements, lifestyle, suspected toxic exposures and a summary of your daily routine. If you choose to make changes to your diet and lifestyle, it is very useful to get a full physical with a complete set of blood biomarkers tested <u>prior</u> to implementing changes. This will serve as your *baseline*. After you make changes to your diet and lifestyle, have these tests repeated so that you and your healthcare provider can track your improvement and make adjustments to any existing medication regimens.

Micronutrient Toxicity

Vitamin and mineral toxicity are adverse toxic effects that result from an abnormally high concentration of the micronutrient. The following are a list of micronutrients that can lead to toxicity. Recommended daily intake (RDI) amounts of micronutrients will vary based upon age and sex. Check the RDI for your particular age range and sex. RDI values change quite frequently during adolescent years. Note the correct RDI age range when looking up your particular needs as many vitamin labels are not specific to age ranges (0 – 6 months, 7 – 12 months, 1 – 3 years, 4 – 8 years, 9 – 13 years, 14 – 18 years, 19 – 50 years, 51 or greater).

Micronutrient Name	Toxic Effect
Vitamin A – Retinol	Headache, peeling of skin, hepatosplenomegaly (simultaneous enlargement of liver and spleen), bone thickening, intracranial hypertension, papilledema (optic disc swelling that is a result of intracranial pressure)
Vitamin B3 – Niacin	Flushing of skin
Vitamin B6 – Pyridoxine, pyridoxal, pyridoxamine	Peripheral neuropathy (peripheral nervous system nerves do not function properly)
Copper (Cu)	Wilson's disease (liver & nervous system toxicity), copper poisoning
Vitamin D	Hypercalcemia (too much calcium

Vitamin D (cont.)	in the blood, pain, weakness, twitching, vomiting), anorexia, renal failure, metastatic calcifications (calcium deposits)
Vitamin E	Easily bleeding
Fluorine (F)	Fluorosis (dental or skeletal discoloration or disturbances), mottling and pitting of permanent teeth, Spinal exostoses (bone tumor of spine)
Iodine (I)	Hyperthyroidism (overactive thyroid – too much thyroid hormones produced – difficulty concentrating, fatigue, frequent bowl movements) or hypothyroidism (too little thyroid hormones produced – depression, fatigue, cold sensitivity)
Iron (Fe)	Hemochromatosis, cirrhosis, diabetes mellitus, skin pigmentation disorder
Manganese (Mn)	Wilson's Disease (liver and nervous system toxicity), Neurological symptoms resembling Parkinson's Disease
Selenium (Se)	Hair loss, abnormal nails, nausea, dermatitis, peripheral neuropathy
Zinc (Zn)	RBC microcytosis, neutropenia, impaired immunity

Chapter Summary

The cause of many of our health issues can and may be traced back to either a single exposure (acute) or a series of exposures (chronic) that can occur over days, months or years. They can also be traced to deficiencies in our bodies. Deficiencies of critical levels of nutrients that allow our body to function properly can also lead to a number of health issues that range from minor to severe and diminish your ability to deal with these toxic exposures. It is vitally important to maintain your body. If you maintain your car or home to keep it running smoothly, make sure you provide a level of care and maintenance for your body too!

REFERENCES & RESOURCES

American Conference of Industrial Hygienists (ACGIH) – www.acgih.org

Ballantyne, B, Marrs, TC & Syverson, T (editors). General and Applied Toxicology. 3rd Edition. 2009. JW Wiley Publishing, United Kingdom.

Centers for Disease Control & Prevention (CDC) – www.cdc.gov

Environment Canada – www.ec.gc.ca

Environmental Protection Agency – www.epa.gov

Food and Drug Administration – www.fda.gov

Klaasen, CD (editor). Cassaret & Doull's Toxicology: The Basic Science of Poisons. 7th Edition. 2007. McGraw-Hill Professional Publishing.

National Organic Program (NOP) – www.ams.usda.gov/nop/

Occupational Safety & Health Administration (OSHA) – www.osha.gov

Omaye, S.T. Food & Nutritional Toxicology. 2004. CRC Press.

TOXNET Toxicology Data Network (National Library of Medicine – National Institutes of Health) s http://toxnet.nlm.nih.gov/

United States Department of Agriculture – www.usda.gov

World Health Organization – www.who.int

ABOUT THE AUTHOR

Dr. Noreen Khan-Mayberry is a toxicologist with a PhD in Environmental Toxicology, MS in Biology and BS in Biology. "Dr. Noreen" is an environmental toxicologist, space toxicologist and technical expert on chemical exposures, food toxicity, environmental health issues, environmental remediation, and green environmental technologies.

Dr. Noreen has spoken nationally and internationally on topics relating to environmental and spaceflight toxicology, reducing exposures to toxins and toxicants, nutritional and food toxicity and leadership. Dr. Noreen's core mission is to take her knowledge as a toxicologist and make it easily understandable to everyone in order to improve their quality of life.

Dr. Noreen is active as a toxicology consultant and has donated countless hours providing free toxicological advice to private groups and concerned individuals to identify sources of toxins and toxicants in their home and work environments. Dr. Noreen was recruited by NASA in 2004 and has served as a federal civil servant since that time. As a Space Toxicologist for NASA, she has developed human health standards and toxicological evaluations for space exploration.

Dr. Noreen's expertise on leadership and finding opportunities in places that may be traditionally closed to women has attracted a wide variety of groups from around the world. Some of Dr. Noreen's honors include being recognized as a 2010 Technology Rising Star and as a distinguished guest speaker at the Women as Global Leaders in Dubai. She also serves as a member of editorial board of The International Journal of Disaster Advances & the Journal of Clinical Toxicology. Dr. Noreen is a Fellow of the International Congress of Disaster Management and is routinely asked to serve as a scientific expert on various media outlets.

www.DoctorNoreen.com

Made in the USA
Lexington, KY
05 January 2014